What can we learn from those pe[...] Jesus? Thanks to Derek Cooper [...] to avoid shaping Jesus according to our expectations rather than as he is presented in the Gospels. I recommend this well-written book to all who want their false assumptions exposed in order to have their faith strengthened and deepened.

—TREMPER LONGMAN III, Robert H. Gundry professor of biblical studies, Westmont College

We've asked ourselves for years, "What would Jesus do?" *Unfollowers* gets me to ask myself "What would *I* do around Jesus?" This question yields a more compelling and convincing insight into my character. Christ compels me through its pages.

—DAVID DRURY, author, speaker, and chief of staff to the General Superintendent of The Wesleyan Church

In this challenging and engaging book, Cooper and Cyzewski help us place ourselves in the shoes of Jesus' original audience. As we engage with the realities of these often-ignored or even despised characters in the Bible and their interactions with Jesus, we find ourselves in their stories and both our faith and our practice is challenged in new ways.

—KATHY ESCOBAR, copastor of The Refuge and author of *Down We Go*

Unfollowers made me laugh . . . and gulp. Weaving biblical observations with contemporary narratives, the authors take readers on a journey of replacing the messiah we create in our own image with the real Sabbath-breaking, wine-making, table-shaking Son of God. If maintaining the status quo is your goal, run—do not walk—away from this book.

—DR. SANDRA GLAHN, associate professor of media arts and worship at Dallas Theological Seminary and author of the Coffee Cup Bible Study series

Unfollowers is only for those brave enough to confront the possibility that Jesus might be calling us to leave our own unfollowing for a life of radical discipleship. Derek Cooper and Ed Cyzewski recapture the prophetic edge of the Gospels by holding up these stories of failure as a mirror into our own hearts. This book has the power to transform where we find ourselves in the biblical story.

—J. R. DANIEL KIRK, associate professor of New Testament, Fuller Theological Seminary

Who wants to focus on the dropouts and doubters? Scripture does. And Cooper and Cyzewski follow the Bible's example, apparently believing the radical notion that all Scripture is inspired and profitable for teaching. They take readers into unexplored areas of the Gospels that are typically ignored, and in doing so enlighten, encourage, and exhort readers into a deeper relationship with their Lord and Master. I have no doubt that readers will profit from their wisdom.

—DAVID T. LAMB, author of *God Behaving Badly*

A jolt for those who are a little too comfortable with the Jesus they think they know.

—JAROD OSBORNE, author of *Jaded Faith*

Ed and Derek open our eyes to a unique and fascinating examination of what a faithful disciple looks like—and from a narrative that most of us have never considered. Beware: This book may cause you to become a follower of the true Messiah!

—JEREMY SUMMERS, author and director of adult spiritual formation of The Wesleyan Church

Many who study the Gospels consider the stories of faithful disciples and followers of Jesus. Few have taken time to examine those who chose not to follow Jesus. In this easily accessible book for pastors and laypeople, the authors help us consider ten types of people who chose not to follow Jesus. This clever book will help you appreciate those who said no to following Jesus so that you may say yes to Jesus in a better way.

—H. DRAKE WILLIAMS, III, Ph.D., academic dean, Tyndale Theological Seminary

We all need help in seeing, loving, trusting, and surrendering. By taking a thoughtful and historical look at the "unfollowers" of Jesus, Derek and Ed help us see Christ clearer, love and trust him more, and freshly surrender our lives to him. By looking at the unfollowers, we learn to follow him closer.

—J. R. WOODWARD, national director of the V3 Church Planting Movement and author of *Creating a Missional Culture*

■UN■FOLLOWERS

UNLIKELY LESSONS ON FAITH FROM THOSE WHO DOUBTED JESUS

Derek Cooper

Ed Cyzewski

wphonline.com

Copyright © 2014 by Derek Cooper and Ed Cyzewski
Published by Wesleyan Publishing House
Indianapolis, Indiana 46250
Printed in the United States of America
ISBN: 978-0-89827-743-2
ISBN (e-book): 978-0-89827-744-9

Library of Congress Cataloging-in-Publication Data

Cooper, Derek, 1978-
  Unfollowers : dropouts, detractors, and doubters of Jesus / Derek Cooper, Ed
Cyzewski.
     pages cm
  ISBN 978-0-89827-743-2
  1. Jesus Christ--Person and offices. 2. Christian biography. 3. Church history.
I. Title.
  BT203.C6675 2014
  232.9'5--dc23
                                        2013033138

All Scripture quotations, unless otherwise indicated, are taken from the Holy
Bible, New International Version®, NIV ®. Copyright ©1973, 1978, 1984, 2011
by Biblica, Inc. Used by permission of Zondervan. All rights reserved worldwide.
www.zondervan.com. The "NIV" and "New International Version" are trademarks
registered in the United States Patent and Trademark Office by Biblica, Inc.

Scripture quotations marked (NLT) are taken from the Holy Bible, New Living
Translation, copyright © 1996, 2004, 2007 by Tyndale House Foundation.
Used by permission of Tyndale House Publishers, Inc., Carol Stream, Illinois
60188. All rights reserved.

Published in association with the literary agency of Credo Communications,
LLC, Grand Rapids, Michigan, www.credocommunications.net.

All rights reserved. No part of this publication may be reproduced, stored in a
retrieval system, or transmitted in any form or by any means—electronic,
mechanical, photocopy, recording, or any other—except for brief quotations
in printed reviews, without the prior written permission of the publisher.

CONTENTS

For a free download of a group study for each chapter,
visit wphresources.com/unfollowers.

PREFACE

Who wrote this book? That is a common question for coauthored projects, and answering it requires a little background.

I (Ed) first thought of this book concept while in seminary, but when I decided to pursue it as a book project, I asked Derek to work with me at a very early point. Since then, Derek and I have shared notes and revised drafts over the years, each chapter representing a blend of our ideas. After we finally put together a proposal, Derek took a scattered set of chapter ideas and systematically combed through the Gospels to make sure we represented as many stories as possible without repeating ourselves. The book has a far sharper focus and more orderly presentation because of his work. Derek also wrote extensive notes for each chapter, providing background information, interpretive options, and application ideas. I used Derek's notes to write each chapter. I also wrote almost all of the short anecdotes and personal stories. Derek reviewed each chapter, removed my puns, and cleaned up any confusing parts. I reviewed Derek's changes, stuck a few puns back in, and smoothed out anything that didn't quite fit.

As a general rule, if you think this book is intelligent and well-researched, you can thank Derek. If you're wondering where a play on words came from, you can thank me.

ACKNOWLEDGEMENTS

ED'S ACKNOWLEDGEMENTS

Kevin Scott of Wesleyan Publishing House took me out for coffee to discuss book ideas. I had a lot of them, but I held one back because I didn't have a good title for it yet. After our coffee had gone cold, I finally mentioned, "There is this project that my friend and I have been working on. I love it, but I can't quite sum it up very well. I need to work with an editor who has a vision for this project." *Unfollowers* was that book project, and I'm grateful that Kevin had the vision and words of encouragement to help make this book a reality. I'm grateful for his support and expertise.

I can't say enough good things about my coauthor, Derek Cooper, even if I can think of some bad things like his love for Dallas sports teams. Derek has added order, insight, and excellent ideas throughout the planning and writing stages. His research and application points are excellent, and I marvel at his time management abilities. He caught large and small mistakes while also providing a firm grasp of how these various stories intersected throughout the Gospels. His appendix that lists every "unfollower" in the Gospels is but a small sample of his conscientious work and knowledge of the Scriptures.

Books aren't written without a strong support network, and my wife, Julie, has been that for me over and over again. Despite her hectic graduate school schedule, she graciously chipped in when deadlines loomed to keep me on task. Writing a book can be a tremendous source of stress, and Julie has been an unwavering source of support, wisdom, and love through it all.

David Drury has been a wonderful encouragement and an early supporter of this book. Matthew Paul Turner routinely offered sage advice. My e-newsletter subscribers read some early chapter drafts and offered great feedback, including Tanya Marlow, John Nunnikhoven, and many others I've surely overlooked. Vince Gierer, Emma Liddle, and several others at St. Paul's Church provided key insights for several chapters, especially for Pilate, Caiaphas, and Judas. My agent Karen Neumair has been beautifully blunt and continually constructive with her feedback.

I'm grateful for the team at WPH who were continually positive and helpful throughout the entire publication process. It's almost like this partnership was predestined.

DEREK'S ACKNOWLEDGEMENTS

In addition to recognizing Karen Neumair, Kevin Scott, and Wesleyan Publishing House, I would like to thank my good friend and coauthor, Ed Cyzewski. In some circles, I have become "that guy" who writes books with some other guy whose name is apparently very hard to pronounce. This book is not going to make things easier. Not only is my coauthor's name still difficult to pronounce, but we have also made up a new word in the title of the book! Either way, I'm delighted to be associated with Ed once again. It's wonderful to have a friend I can bounce ideas off of, even ones that turn out to not be very good. In this case, we are excited to present a topic that we have tossed back and forth for some time. Here's to the next book, Ed!

I would also like to thank the beautiful and kind woman who is my wife, Barb. Because the ink in my pen would dry before I could finish saying enough good things about Barb, I will just give her my thanks and all the love that resides in my heart. It is nothing but joy to live life with her and our three children. Thank you for your love and support!

INTRODUCTION

A MESSIAH WHO DIDN'T FIT THE JOB DESCRIPTION

If I made a list of what a modern-day messiah should do, I would create a balanced, sensible list. I'd like a messiah to be powerful enough to solve my problems and defeat evil. He would challenge me to change my life, but at my own pace.

I assume that any messiah would rescue the faithful from hell. He'd also save the environment from destruction. He'd shop at thrift stores and serve up fair trade, organic coffee—certainly light roast. My kind of messiah would write on a regular basis, enjoy gardening, and squeeze in service to others when possible. I suppose watching hockey would be optional. I'd also keep the part about turning water into wine. In short, my description of a messiah is basically an awesome version of me who bears minimal resemblance to the Jesus of the Gospels.

My list probably sounds pretty ridiculous to you. That's because you know that Jesus would never resemble the character I described in my list. You have your own list of expectations for a modern-day messiah. Other versions of the messiah croon old hymns, spend hours studying the Bible, drink craft beers while chatting about theology, start evangelistic conversations everywhere they go, play soccer, compare everything spiritual to the military, lift their hands during worship, advocate for political reforms, go on mission trips, or reward the faithful with fancy cars and big homes.

To one degree or another, we all imagine that Jesus looks just like us and wants the same things as us.

My friend Chad has a picture of a smiling and winking Jesus figurine on his blog giving the thumbs-up to all who drop by for a visit. When I think about Jesus dropping by my home and learning about what I do, I tend to imagine him looking something like that. We'd chat for a bit and then, with a smile, a wink, and a thumbs-up, he'd walk out the door to tell my neighbors across the alley to let their barking dog inside. "Keep up the good work!" he yells to me from the street as he walks away.

My smiling, winking Jesus met his match one day. In fact, while in seminary, I realized that Jesus may not have spent too much time smiling and winking at people like me. Obsessed with the right answers, short on service to others, and prone to judgment, I saw that I had far more in common with the Pharisees and Sadducees who opposed Jesus.

WHO WAS ON JESUS' SIDE?

It's never a good day when you realize you have quite a bit in common with the villains of the Bible. It's even worse when you've made this discovery while in seminary.

I used to always identify with the heroes in the Bible. Who wants to be the villain? If ten out of twelve spies didn't want to invade Canaan, I'd surely be one of the two who trusted God to lead the way. If the entire nation of Israel turned to Baal worship, I'd be hiding in a cave with Elijah's seven thousand faithful Israelites. If nine of ten healed lepers failed to follow Jesus, I'd be the one who returned to say thank you.

It never occurred to me that I could have anything in common with the crowds who yawned at or mocked Jesus' message. Even worse than that, how could I have any similarities with the opponents of Jesus?

The more I considered what kind of messiah I expected to find in the Bible, the more I saw the ways I'd misconstrued Jesus and remade him into my image. I didn't have all that much in common with Jesus. In fact, I had way more in common with the Pharisees. The Pharisees had very set beliefs about who God is, what God does, and God's plans for the future. They knew the Bible way better than I ever will. If anyone could be described as eager for God to show up, they've certainly got me beat since I don't live under a brutal Roman military occupation. Every time I found the Pharisees, I tried to stick myself in their shoes—or sandals if you will. Each time, their sandals felt eerily familiar and comfortable.

After reading the Bible from their perspective, I began to understand them, though of course I didn't have a "pro-Pharisee" reading of the Bible. I didn't make a WWPD bracelet. They certainly weren't misunderstood heroes by any means. But I could see their airtight theology, how they expected the Messiah to be just like themselves, and how Jesus completely defied their expectations. I understood what they expected God to do, and how Jesus just couldn't work as the Messiah in light of that. When they stood on the sidelines criticizing the miracles and compassion of Jesus, I saw people who applied the Bible a little too ignorantly. The more I observed their behavior, the more I saw myself.

The Pharisees, like all of us, apparently expected a messiah who looked like themselves and fit the job description they'd created over time. When Jesus challenged their conception of what a messiah is and does—even overturning their dearly held practices and beliefs—they refused to follow someone who didn't affirm themselves or their beliefs. Just as I'd created a winking and smiling Jesus giving me a thumbs-up, the Pharisees imagined the Messiah would give them a pat on the back. When the Messiah didn't look like them, they dismissed him. In that moment of revelation in seminary, I had to decide whether I wanted to follow the Jesus in the Gospels who healed, challenged, and blessed, or settle for a messiah who is nothing more than a slightly better caricature of myself.

Reeling in shock from the loss of my lighthearted thumbs-up Jesus, I mentioned my struggles in an online chat with a friend. He wasn't surprised. "Yeah," he typed. "I often wonder if I'm the kind of guy who would have mocked Jesus. That haunts me for sure." The thought of identifying with the mockers of Jesus, someone other than the Pharisees, opened up a whole new line of thinking. The religion scholars weren't the only ones who had a tough time figuring out Jesus. I realized that there's much more to the story of those who didn't follow Jesus than my affinity with the Pharisees. In fact, the Gospels are filled with their stories, even if these "unfollowers" merely lurk in the background of the stories, never moving to center stage.

During Jesus' time, there was never a unified view of the Messiah. Instead, there were many different groups of Jews in Jesus' day that held contrary views of what it even meant to be a Jew. Nevertheless, it is clear from the Gospels that Jesus consistently defied the people's expectations of what the Messiah would be and do. Apparently, for instance, no one expected a messiah to heal or do anything perceived as "work" on the Sabbath, hang out with notorious sinners, forgive women caught in adultery, violate hand-washing traditions, downplay the importance of the temple, peacefully resist the despised Roman overlords, or insult the religious authorities. In short, although there was never a single poster in the Holy Land titled "The Job Description of the Messiah," whatever expectations the Jews had about the Messiah were different from Jesus' actions.

Besides these expectations that kept people from following Jesus, I began to notice many other reasons people chose to "unfollow" Jesus. I saw people who were busy, skeptical, greedy, and distracted by their own religious practices and preferences. I saw people—good, honest, hard-working people—who remained in the background of the gospel stories, observing from the crowds but never committing to become a disciple. In fact, most of the crowds in the Gospels could be described as rather indifferent, not choosing to follow or oppose Jesus but always grateful for a free lunch or a nifty miracle story. They were committed to reading the Scriptures in the synagogue and waiting for the Messiah, but they didn't really want to disrupt their lives. They certainly weren't going to take any risks for the sake of this new miracle worker allegedly born out of wedlock. Jesus was merely a nice carpenter who hailed from a completely insignificant village in the northern part of Israel that was far removed from the religious and political epicenter in Jerusalem. Many of the people who listened to Jesus didn't necessarily oppose Jesus, but then again, they didn't want him making their lives any more complicated than they already were. Some regarded him as a great healer and magician, but few were willing to follow him at all costs.

While the Gospels share stories of successful disciples and tell us to follow Jesus, they also tell us quite a lot about the expectations that can keep us from truly knowing Jesus and the obstacles that can prevent us from following him. With only the success stories of the Bible in mind, I quickly projected myself alongside Jesus—a Savior who was all smiles and thumbs-up. This is a natural trap that anyone can fall into.

I'd been missing out on the lessons from the non-disciples, those who unfollowed Jesus. Their stories provided the perfect foil for the faithful disciples, creating a contrast that helped me see my own expectations and potential barriers that could keep me from following Jesus. Years of studying the people who got it right only resulted in convincing me that *I* was right. Studying the people who got it wrong provided the most effective insight into the flaws of my own heart. Once I knew what a failed disciple looked like, I saw the faithful disciples with new eyes.

Though I'm convinced that I'm still on Jesus' side, the majority of the people in the gospel stories would have said they were on God's side. When I assert that I can figure out how to follow Jesus and that I can't possibly repeat their mistakes, I'm reminded that Jesus criticized his audience for mourning at the tombs of the prophets while rejecting the fulfillment of their messages. In other words, it's possible to be on the same literal page as God in the Scriptures and not be on the same page as God. Though seeing, they didn't perceive its significance. Sinful patterns had infiltrated their lives and certain messianic expectations had clouded their minds, preventing them from joining God when he showed up among them.

The more I examined myself in light of the Pharisees—the indifferent, busy, and even hostile opponents of Jesus—the more I noticed troubling trends in my own life. I could be a critical, theological judge of Christians who were doing much more good for the kingdom than I was. I could judge people who advocated for the poor because they were relying on government over the church. I could underestimate the power of God. I could let doubts cloud my ability to hear God's voice in my daily life. I could ignore the restoring work of God around me. I could let my own priorities and dreams choke out the joy of knowing Jesus.

If we are made whole by confessing our sins to God, we need to detect them first. That's what makes the New Testament so fascinating to me: So many people didn't realize they were missing the Messiah due to their expectations, greed, indifference, fear, ambition, and beliefs. I'm not good at detecting my own flaws. Who wants to look at all of that?

My weakness at self-examination makes these stories all the more necessary for today. When we place ourselves in the shoes of Jesus' original audience, a strange feeling comes over us: We start to relate to them. When we empathize with their stories, we can start to identify the sins creeping up in our lives and confess them. A story about Caiaphas won't teach us all that much about salvation, but his story has much to teach us about divided loyalties and the subtle ways hypocrisy twists good things into evil. When we encounter sin in full bloom in these stories, we have a kind of microscope through which we can examine the gravity of sin, seeing it for what it is, lest we go easy on ourselves. Sin is never a small matter. Doubt may be part of our growth process, but if left unaddressed, it can undermine our faith over time. Greed can skew our priorities to the point that we exploit others in ways we never could imagine. Judgment can cut us off from the love and healing of God. Theology can be used as a tool to divide and condemn people who may otherwise be our allies.

Let's face it, if God is working miracles, healing broken lives, and restoring justice in our world, we don't want to miss out on it. The disciples in the New Testament were on the front lines with the intense work of ministry, setting aside time for Jesus, and letting him guide them. The unfollowers sat back, avoiding direct involvement with that nice young carpenter from Galilee.

The first step in learning from those who unfollowed Jesus is entering into their world, understanding what they wanted out of life and the challenges they faced. We need to move beyond vague character sketches, stock characters, or one-dimensional renderings where the unfollowers merely serve as foils to the true disciples. From the perspective of the unfollowers, there were plenty of good reasons to avoid Jesus. If we can't understand these reasons and apply them to our own lives, what makes us so sure we'll do any better at following Jesus? How can we be sure we'll overcome the same obstacles that tripped up the majority of the people in Jesus' original audience? Before we can ask why each individual character failed to follow Jesus, we need to attempt to see the time of Christ through their eyes and the events that shaped their hopes for a specific kind of messiah.

THE WORST HISTORY LESSON EVER

History wasn't the most cheerful subject for children growing up in Israel. Slavery, wandering in the desert, the constant threat of war, exile, poverty, and then exploitation by the Greek and Roman empires made for one tragic story after another. We're not talking about a recession or a bad season of network television. During the exile, an entire nation was uprooted from their homes, moved to a foreign land, and then experienced the constant threat of attack and oppression. A cross-country move in America is hard enough without a soldier jamming his sword in your back along the way. The history of Israel had some high points for sure, but the majority of Israelites faced extreme suffering, death, and exploitation at the hands of powerful invading armies from Egypt, Assyria, Babylon, Greece, and Rome. Their little slice of land happened to be a valuable overland trading route that no empire could resist.

Though God delivered the Israelites on many occasions, hardships and tragedies littered the history of the Israelites right up to the Roman military occupation of Israel. The only faint glimmer of post-exile hope came when Judas Maccabeus led a successful rebellion against the Greek rulers who had banned observance of the Jewish Law, killed many Jews, and even defiled the temple.

The Maccabees family established the fragile Hasmonean dynasty that was prone to intrigue and infighting. This fledgling state hardly realized the hopes spoken of in the prophets and must have proven a tremendous disappointment. In the midst of military victory and Jewish autonomy, God still did not return to his suffering people. Rather, internal fighting threatened the Hasmonean rule until the rising Roman Empire took over at the invitation of one Jewish party with designs on the throne. Herod the Great eventually established himself as Rome's representative to rule the land of Israel, the very same Herod who met the magi, killed infants, and drowned relatives in his various swimming pools.

From the exile to the rule of Rome, Israel endured a series of crushing defeats, unimaginable oppression, and heartbreaking disappointments. The people of Israel longed for the return of God to the land, bringing them freedom, justice, and peace, while driving out and punishing their enemies. The Jewish people in the audience of John the Baptist and Jesus didn't just expect a messiah who would rule as king; they expected nothing less than the dramatic, world-changing return of God to rule as king.

Much has been written about the Pharisees who emerged after the exile as interpreters of Scripture and who tried to put Israel back on the right course after suffering such severe retribution for its sins. The wounds of the exile ran deep, leaving scars on these people, driving them to rigorous study of the Scriptures. They refused to make the same mistakes as their ancestors who rejected and even killed the prophets. In many ways, they heroically picked up the pieces and tried to move forward under trying circumstances.

If you distilled the mission of the Pharisees, you might say they had to prepare the people for God's coming—a return announced by the Messiah. They taught obedience to the law and looked forward to the Messiah's arrival as a result of obedience to that law. There is a tradition among Jews to this day that if every Jew keeps just one perfect Sabbath at the same time, the Messiah will come back. While we read about the Pharisees and Sadducees raking Jesus over the coals for his supposed violations of the Jewish Law, in the background, driving their exacting theology and application, is their role in preparing the people for the return of God. They gave their lives to this work. They studied the law so they would receive the Messiah with open arms.

After years of waiting and studying the Scriptures, the religious leaders of Israel conspired to kill Jesus.

WHAT KEEPS US FROM FOLLOWING JESUS?

The Gospels tell the kinds of stories that should keep us up at night. When the people who knew the Bible best couldn't recognize the coming of God in their midst, we have a kind of theological thriller that is quite terrifying for those committed to studying and obeying the Scriptures. When the disciples learned that the religious teachers of their day couldn't cut it in God's kingdom they asked, "Then who can be saved?" Can you feel the tension in that question? Even the disciples who spent every day with Jesus needed a lot of time and explanation before they figured out Jesus. If that's the case, then what makes us so sure we won't miss him too? Whether our expectations or sinful habits obstruct our view, there are plenty of ways to overlook Jesus.

We need to place ourselves in the shoes of Jesus' audience and figure out how he defied the expectations of his audience and follow that with the hard work of opening our lives to the Spirit of God. As we encounter Jesus and his unexpected challenges to our lives, let's ask the Spirit to convict, change, and renew us. In addition, we should pay particular attention to the kind of people Jesus sought out, those he called blessed, and those who received and clung to his message.

In other words, if we read the Gospels and find a Jesus who isn't all that demanding, challenging, or countercultural (a Jesus who is merely a superior version of ourselves), then there's a good chance we aren't meeting the Jesus that the gospel writers had in mind. The audience of Jesus was often puzzled, challenged, or disturbed by his words and actions. What are the odds that we are more clever or knowledgeable than the Pharisees and teachers of the law? Could we desire God's Messiah more than people who lived under Roman oppression? While we have the advantage of the Holy Spirit among us, the Gospels remind us that it's very easy to miss Jesus. Finding him will take both careful thought and prayerful meditation on what God is teaching us.

This is a somewhat unconventional approach to discipleship. I'm suggesting that we look for the places in the Gospels where Jesus' listeners missed the point or found Jesus difficult to accept and that we contrast these unfollowers with faithful disciples.

Part of our task will be to slow down our readings of the Gospels and ponder the details, asking why Jesus challenged his original audience to rethink their religious customs, their expectations of the Messiah, and their approach to sinners. In a sense, we have become too familiar with the Gospels, overlooking events, sayings, and reactions that should give us pause. Keep in mind that John, the beloved disciple, said the world could not hold all of the books that could be written about all that Jesus said and did. Every single detail in the Gospels is crucial, demanding slow and careful readings.

Jesus told his followers:

Not everyone who says to me, "Lord, Lord," will enter the kingdom of heaven, but only the one who does the will of my Father who is in heaven. Many will say to me on that day, "Lord, Lord, did we not prophesy in your name and in your name drive out demons and in your name perform many miracles?" Then I will tell them plainly, "I never knew you. Away from me, you evildoers!" Therefore everyone who hears these words of mine and puts them into practice is like a wise man who built his house on the rock. (Matt. 7:21–24)

There are two key lessons that we should keep in mind from this passage. First, Jesus made it very clear that some who claim him as their Lord and Savior don't actually know him and will even be cast away as evildoers. Even with miracles and prophecies to their credit, they have missed out on knowing Jesus and living in righteous obedience to him. Second, in this passage, Jesus had been talking about trees bearing fruit and he would move on to describe a house built on a rock—both metaphors illustrate the importance of putting the words of Jesus into practice.

Jesus called his audience to move beyond merely understanding his words, calling him Lord, or even performing miracles. He was looking for people who would dig into his message, grasp its meaning, and then engage in the hard work of putting it into practice. Our comfort in our own culture and our familiarity with the story of Jesus can tame his message and rob us of the opportunity to encounter him and put his words into practice. In fact, if we don't take the time to understand his message and to carefully put it into practice, he said we are foolish and can expect nothing from God.

There are consequences for missing Jesus, real consequences that demand a pause to evaluate our understanding of who Jesus really is and what he expects of us. However, if we can let Jesus disrupt the barriers that keep us from him, we will experience the abundant life that he promised. The cost of failure is steep, but the rewards are beyond what we can imagine. Learning from the mistakes of those who ignored and rejected Jesus will require humility and faith that God's Spirit can guide his people to right belief and faithful practice. As we look at the ways Jesus' original audience missed him, I pray that our own lives will remain open to the promptings of God's Spirit so that we will be able to follow him faithfully today without hindrance.

Our journey begins with an unusual man who became the focal point of messianic hope at the time of Jesus. After a miraculous birth, his life calling became announcing the arrival of the Messiah. After pointing to Jesus, God himself confirmed that he had pointed out the right man as the Messiah. How this man ended up harboring doubts is the subject of our first story.

■1 JOHN THE BAPTIST

A MESSIAH NO ONE EXPECTED

In the spring of 1738, John Wesley returned to England after a failed ministry in the colony of Georgia. To say Wesley's ministry "failed" understates his situation. His ministry had been a complete and utter fiasco that included a broken engagement, lawsuits, strife within his congregation, and failed outreach to the Native Americans. As his former fiancée's new husband tried to drag him into court, Wesley could only hope to escape his pastoral post by jumping on a ship bound for England.

While searching for answers, Wesley began to spend time in Moravian meetings—a group that emphasized personal holiness and commitment to reading and practicing Scripture. At a Moravian meeting in Aldersgate, Wesley felt his heart "strangely warmed" during an exposition of the book of Romans. In the years that followed, Wesley looked back at this moment as the turning point for his ministry. As he finally grasped the significance of salvation by faith, he found a true catalyst for life change and for his ministry. Wesley didn't just revolutionize his personal approach to holy living and preaching; he founded small groups and commissioned preachers to carry this message throughout England and deep into the new American colonies. His orderly approach to holiness became known as Methodism, but you can see the growth of Wesley's ministry in a wide variety of Christian denominations to this day.

We've all been "strangely warm" at times. Perhaps a fever knocks us out or we forget to turn down the heat at night. Why would anyone base an entire ministry on a moment that seems so arbitrary? Whatever God did to the heart of John Wesley, it served as confirmation that he needed to change his approach to God and his ministry among those around him. Perhaps he was so thirsty for any kind of experience of God that a warm heart was all he needed.

I have many friends who have shared similar experiences with Wesley. They've described the presence of God as a profound sense of peace, while others have literally wiped sweat off their brows from the "heat" of God's presence. I haven't personally felt the heat of God, but I have experienced the cleansing sorrow of repentance and indescribable joy when I had a kind of vision of God's present kingdom in this world. It's anyone's guess why some people have these experiences and others don't or why they differ so widely from one person to another. But the point is that God stepped into their lives at a particular moment and gave them a sign they could hang onto before making a significant change. Wesley's experience of forgiveness and hope may not strike us as all that impressive in retrospect. We may even be a little bit skeptical. However, it was enough to spark new life in a discouraged preacher. When God needs to unveil his salvation to a discouraged nation, we shouldn't be surprised to find that he brings a whole lot more than some heat.

WOULD YOU TRUST AN ANGEL?
The Angel Made Me Do It

My own experiences of God's presence pale in comparison to the circumstances surrounding the birth of John the Baptist. John's father, Zechariah, wasn't just a respected priest. Due to a series of significant events, the people of his time recognized that God planned to do something extraordinary with Zechariah's family. As he and his wife, Elizabeth, prayed for a child into their old age, they watched their hopes fade with each passing year. But their future was about to dramatically change.

When Zechariah took his turn to serve at the temple, he drew the significant lot to burn incense behind the curtain in the Holy of Holies. This was important enough, but then an angel appeared to him, predicting that he and his wife would conceive a son and name him John. Best yet, John would carry the spirit and power of Elijah, preparing the people of Israel for the Lord. Even if Zechariah didn't believe the angel at first, his loss of speech until John's circumcision ceremony provided enough confirmation about the role of God that everyone in Judea began talking about this baby. By the time they completed the ceremony, John and his family became the talk of the town. This wasn't just notable in and of itself because of the angel's appearance. The story of an elderly couple conceiving a child carried strong overtones from the story of Abraham and Sarah. Everyone would have noted it. What was God preparing to do with his people?

John's miraculous conception, angelic announcement, and father's long prophetic oracle about his ministry supercharged the anticipation of everyone in Judea. How would the spirit of Elijah manifest itself in this child? Would the Messiah come now? Is this child the Messiah? John grew up surrounded by these stories and subsequent speculation about God's plan for his life. His destiny had been handed to him from the start of his life: He would serve as the next Elijah.

Can you imagine the conversations that must have surrounded John at family events as he grew up? Friends and family must have told him over and over again about the angel appearing to his father, his mother's miraculous conception, and his father's nine months of silence followed by a long prophetic poem. I wonder if John felt so much pressure to become a prophet that he ran away to the desert to eat grasshoppers and honey.

Whatever John thought of this, Zechariah had foretold that John would be a prophet who declared the salvation of God's people—the end of the exile. In other words, John was in charge of preparing the way for the Messiah much like Elijah had prepared the way for Elisha. John not only moved into the wilderness to prepare the way for the Lord, he also looked the part of Elijah with his simple camel hair wardrobe and fiery confrontation with Jewish leaders.

John knew from Isaiah that the place to prepare for God's coming was out in the wilderness. In fact, Rome's puppet rulers were always on the lookout for messianic movements, so the wilderness made sense practically as well. The location of John's ministry would have called to mind the exodus experience of Israel—moving from the wilderness to the Promised Land through the Jordan River. The Jews of this time were reenacting the exodus by confessing their sins and undergoing baptism. They did this as a way to hasten God's return to Israel as the rightful king.

Baptism was typically reserved for Gentile converts to Judaism, so the implications of Jews undergoing a baptism of repentance symbolized a commitment to once again live as God's people. John structured his life so that he could live as a prophet—hearing from God, setting himself apart from the world, and living simply, lest anything crowd out God's voice. God spoke and then John set out with his message of hope that the time of suffering and exile was about to end.

At this point in the story, everything seemed to be lining up with everyone's expectations and the Scriptures. An Elijah appeared in the wilderness, and the people responded with repentance. Much like the prophets before him, John called the people to interact with one another justly, to right wrongs, and to remember that God could cut off his "chosen people" should they refuse to repent.

When Jesus arrived on the banks of the Jordan, John baptized him, and then God showed up with a thundering confirmation of Jesus and a dove descending upon him. Though many continued to follow John for years after the appearance of Jesus, John made it clear that Jesus must increase while he decreased. His mission was complete.

Or was it?

While everyone expected Jesus to bring the rule of God back to Israel and to end the exile, Jesus didn't challenge the pagan rulers as anticipated, and he regularly offended the Jewish religious leaders. No one could deny that Jesus had performed many miracles, but he refused to confirm that he was the Messiah either verbally or through a miraculous sign such as calling down fire from the heavens. Jesus always let his audience interpret his signs for themselves. What kind of a leader was this?

Though Jesus certainly helped many people and garnered wide-spread enthusiasm, he hadn't changed very much in Israel other than healing and feeding some people. But even those people whom Jesus fed continued in poverty as before, and the Roman rulers still defiled the land with their oppressive treatment of locals and their unwelcomed occupation of Israel. This was not the way anyone expected God to return. What was a prophet to do?

John believed very deeply that the Messiah would bring righteousness to the land, and he knew that the Messiah was present. Therefore, it's likely that he became bolder with his message. Besides calling the Pharisees and Sadducees a brood of snakes, he also challenged the morality of King Herod. Herod responded by imprisoning John. As the days and months in prison dragged on, John hit a low point. Was he wrong about Jesus? Why would the Messiah leave him in prison without challenging the rulers and authorities? Had he baptized the wrong person?

When Doubts Distract Us from God

Though John saw that the way to prepare for God's coming began in the wilderness, he didn't realize that Jesus would continue to work on the margins in the wilderness and in the relative obscurity of Galilee. Though many came to see him, Jesus did not begin his ministry by directly challenging the rulers of his time. Nor did he immediately rush toward the cities to confront widespread injustice and abuse. When the authorities sought to kill Jesus, it wasn't because he was trying to take their jobs, but because he was initiating a completely different approach to God and power that undermined the existing order and threatened to stir the populace to revolt.

When John spoke of the coming Messiah, he used powerful apocalyptic language that described God's coming judgment of the ungodly: "I baptize you with water. But one who is more powerful than I will come, the straps of whose sandals I am not worthy to untie. He will baptize you with the Holy Spirit and fire. His winnowing fork is in his hand to clear his threshing floor and to gather the wheat into his barn, but he will burn up the chaff with unquenchable fire" (Luke 3:16–17). John didn't see Jesus bringing about the kind of repentance and judgment you would expect during the day of the Lord.

Though Jesus spoke strongly on some occasions, his ministry was hardly the game changer that anyone expected. Instead of a winnowing fork, Jesus gave the people bread and fish. In fact, we might say that Jesus was a disappointment for John and his disciples. Later in the book of Acts, we read that John the Baptist still had followers throughout the Mediterranean region. It seems that while John announced the coming of the Messiah, many people didn't think Jesus was the right choice. As John sat in prison and listened for developments about Jesus, he harbored his own doubts.

When John sent some of his own disciples to ask Jesus about his doubts, he was given a characteristic response from Jesus:

When the men [John's disciples] came to Jesus, they said, "John the Baptist sent us to you to ask, 'Are you the one who is to come, or should we expect someone else?'" At that very time Jesus cured many who had diseases, sicknesses and evil spirits, and gave sight to many who were blind. So he replied to the messengers, "Go back and report to John what you have seen and heard: The blind receive sight, the lame walk, those who have leprosy are cleansed, the deaf hear, the dead are raised, and the good news is proclaimed to the poor. Blessed is anyone who does not stumble on account of me." (Luke 7:20–23)

Rather than receiving a straight yes or no from Jesus, John was forced to rethink his concept of what exactly a messiah is and does. While Jesus performed miracles and healed many people, John was looking for him to usher in the visible rule of God and to bring judgment on the ungodly. He wanted to see fire come down from heaven and consume the unfruitful trees that so pervasively littered God's forest. Instead, Jesus defined the coming of God's kingdom as preaching the good news to the poor, healing the sick, and raising the dead. God was beginning to repair the world's brokenness from the bottom up, but the people who had set themselves apart by observing the law were expecting more.

John didn't see how a real messiah could have so much power and yet hold it back. Didn't Jesus see the injustice and afflictions brought on the people of Israel? Wasn't he disgusted by the rampant immorality of their Jewish "king," Herod? Didn't Jesus have the ability to radically change the corrupt rulers of the land? What happened to the fire and the winnowing fork?

Even more perplexing for John may have been the way the angel's prediction for his life had played out. Wasn't he supposed to have "the spirit and power of Elijah" (Luke 1:17)? The spirit and the power behind Elijah sustained him in a widow's home, along a desert stream, and on a wind-swept mountain. When Ahab and Jezebel threatened Elijah's life, God intervened and saved him. If Herod stood for the new Ahab, and John was fulfilling the role of Elijah, didn't it make sense for him to speak out against his wickedness? And if Jesus was the Messiah, why wasn't he intervening to bring about God's salvation to him and the rest of the people in Israel?

While we have no concrete evidence that John stopped believing Jesus was the Messiah, we also don't know how John responded to the message from Jesus. The last we hear of John is that he had some doubts to work through about Jesus. Soon after that, Herod executed John for criticizing his wife and his illicit marriage to her. Such an end to the story of John is chilling. A story that begins with such hope in the deliverance of God ends in tragedy and despair.

Here was the man set apart from his conception to announce the return of God. From his childhood on through adulthood John had the confirmation of his calling in place from both an angel and his father's prophecy. In response to a direct message from God, he journeyed into the wilderness to begin announcing the return of God. If anyone had a reason for confidence in finding the Messiah, it was John—that was the calling for his entire life. That he came so close to unfollowing Jesus should warn us against thinking we could never miss the work of God among us today.

WHAT DO WE EXPECT FROM JESUS?

While we hope for the best in John's story, we don't know whether he ever made sense of his calling and the work of Jesus. He had a miraculous birth, an angel's prediction, and a prophecy from his father, and yet Jesus still left him uncertain. There were plenty of others in the Gospels who wrestled with the same things as John. Jesus' own mother struggled to accept her Son's calling, even trying to stop his ministry because she and his brothers suspected he'd lost his mind. Thankfully, we learn that Mary was among the followers of Jesus in the upper room during Pentecost. She eventually came around to believe the incredible truth that her Son was actually the Messiah.

Even with angelic visions and prophecies, the people closest to Jesus struggled to believe. This trend suggests that no matter how "close" we may think we are to Jesus, we can still run the risk of missing him.

Believing in the Wrong "Jesus"

The life of John reminds us that Jesus can surprise even the most prepared person. Once we begin to attach expectations and assumptions to Jesus, we may place ourselves in a position to miss him. It's easy to impose our own expectations upon Jesus, creating different portraits where he's an ideal business man, a gentle pushover, or a tough, macho man.

Each portrait of Jesus picks up on a different element of his story, inflates it, and covers up the more complex features of Jesus and his ministry. Businessman Jesus turns Jesus into a shrewd manager of people and resources who skillfully builds an effective inner circle of followers. The gentle Jesus welcomes all, holds back on judgment, and bestows unlimited grace and patience on sinners who are never empowered to change. Macho Jesus gets tough on his opponents, thrashes bad theology, and warns his audience of God's coming wrath.

Just as John made assumptions based both on Scripture and expectations circulating at his time, we also construct pictures of who Jesus is, what he does, and how we should respond to him based on the snippets of Jesus' story that resonate with our preferences. Throughout the Gospels, Jesus ran into expectations and categories that he continuously challenged or subverted. He met expectations in part, but he also pursued different directions than his audience anticipated.

Jesus certainly came with a kind of winnowing fork and fire, but he didn't bring the kind of final judgment his audience expected. He came to bring salvation, to expose the hearts of many, and to eventually baptize his followers with fire and the Holy Spirit on Pentecost. He inaugurated the kingdom of God, but he started from the bottom, in the margins, and in obscurity. His kingdom was like slow-moving yeast working its way through bread dough.

Besides missing Jesus, it's also easy to miss what Jesus wants to accomplish in our lives. John didn't expect his ministry to end in a dank prison cell. Many of the expected outcomes for John's ministry never materialized. We can fall into the same trap for ourselves. Successful Christians supposedly have large churches, political influence, or spiritually victorious lives. We forget that sometimes God works through slow-moving, bottom-up means, even when there's an ongoing struggle with sin or a lack of outward signs of progress. Incredible growth may happen at times, but God's standards rarely become standardized. Faithfulness to God's calling often looks quite different than we expect.

Perhaps God has called us to minister in obscurity or in the margins. Perhaps taking a stand for Christ requires stepping back from the public spotlight and serving among those who cannot raise our profiles in a particular job or in a particular neighborhood. When we become attached to a particular portrait of Jesus, a particular way that ministry needs to happen, or particular goals that we expect, then we may end up rejecting the work God is doing around us, missing out on the blessings and joys he wants to pour on us. As we seek to know Jesus, we need to balance what we know of him with what we still need to discover. We balance our certainty with the expectation that God can always bring fresh insights to us.

How Jesus Changed My Picture of Himself

When I started attending seminary, I wanted nothing more than to become a church-planting pastor, imagining that God could only use me in a leadership capacity on the staff of a church. When I finally joined a church part-time, I quickly realized that God had not called me into that kind of ministry. For two years, I tried to make it work, but there was no escaping the fact that God had different plans.

I spent four years fighting God about his plans for my life after graduating from seminary. One night a friend prayed over me that God was preparing me for "something" and just the thought of having a calling was more than I could bear. I craved it in my time of uncertainty and wandering. I doubled over weeping as I confessed my expectations and stubbornness. I had been trying to cram God's plans for me into my own definitions of success. Over the following years, God brought me to a place of accepting his plans and expectations for my life. Although your experiences with and expectations of God are not necessarily the same as mine, I think many of us can relate to John the Baptist as he looked at Jesus and thought to himself, "This is not what I had in mind."

There are men and women today trying to make the best of difficult situations at work or in particular neighborhoods because they believe God has to use them in that particular place. They become attached to their goals and expected outcomes without realizing that God may have something different in mind. Some may be working in a church and need to get out. Some may need to give up on their careers to embrace a specific calling in a Christian ministry. Some may need to commit themselves to their secular jobs to be faithful to God. Some may need to accept staying put, while others need to break out of a rut and dream of something new. A close friend of mine and his wife discovered that God was actually calling them to minister in their hometown back in the United States rather than serving on the mission field.

Finding the way of Jesus isn't always easy. Sometimes God has to realign our expectations according to his plans before he can use us in ways that bring blessings to others, as well as ourselves.

PERSEVERANCE ISN'T ABOUT WHERE WE START

Sometimes we just want a sign that things are going to work out and that we're on the right track. Will I find God's calling for my life? Will I be a good parent? Will I reach all of my career goals? Will I stay faithful to God until the end? John had a word of assurance for his life. God's plan was spread out before him, and he still struggled to follow it. Perhaps we need to be careful what we wish for.

While a powerful prophecy or moment of conversion can jumpstart us and send us on the right path toward God, persevering has never been about starting well. John Wesley didn't rely on his warm heart to sustain himself throughout his ministry. He cultivated spiritual practices and met with Christians who could help keep him accountable each week. His expectations hindered his ability to see Jesus as the Messiah. The same could be true for us. If we aren't cultivating spiritual practices that enable us to hear God speak today, we may end up looking for God in the wrong places.

Jesus had many surprises in store for his audience in the Gospels and has plenty more for us in the present. If John the Baptist was the most likely person to recognize Jesus as the Messiah, then perhaps the people of Nazareth who knew Jesus best were the second most likely. Sadly, their response to Jesus moved far beyond uncertainty or doubt.

◼2 THE TOWNSPEOPLE OF NAZARETH

A MESSIAH WHO IS EXTRAORDINARY

The family of Qamar Zia regretted sending her to a Christian school in northern India after a teacher introduced her to the Bible and she converted to Christianity in 1946. When Zia's family moved to Pakistan during the partition of 1947, she took the bold step of contacting a missionary named Marian Laugesen in Karachi, who supplied her with a New Testament. The faith of Zia's high school teachers stuck with her as she committed herself to reading the Bible in secret.

Conflict erupted with Zia's family seven years after her conversion when they began to pressure her to marry a Muslim man. She fled back to Karachi where she reconnected with Laugesen and worked in an orphanage. In a move that further severed ties with her family, Zia took the name Esther John.

Even though she had run away, her family continued to pressure her to return and marry. They refused to accept her conversion, so Esther fled to Sahiwal. She found work in a mission hospital, but her true calling was teaching. She began taking classes in the United Bible Training Centre in 1956, and three years later, she moved to Chichawatni where she worked with American missionaries.

A brave and capable teacher, Esther John traveled from one village to another on her bicycle to teach women to read, share the gospel, and work in the cotton fields. Throughout her mission work, her family continued to reach out to her, sometimes with a hope for reconciliation and other times with a significant amount of tension. Unfortunately, they weren't the only ones who opposed Esther John's work. As word spread about this brilliant missionary, radicals began to plot her death. On February 2, 1960, an extremist brutally murdered her in her sleep.[1]

Esther John remained faithful in the face of opposition from her family, neighbors, and religious radicals. She chose to count herself among God's family rather than cave to the norms and expectations of her biological family.

The story about Jesus' homecoming to Nazareth taps into the tension that surfaces when a shift in religious beliefs hits a tight-knit family and community. But Jesus wasn't just asking his family and hometown friends to accept his own changes in religious beliefs. Jesus asked his hometown to change their perceptions about God, salvation, and who God wants to save. By the time Jesus rocked their world with his message, many openly asked, "Who are you to lecture us about God?"

YOU CAN'T GO HOME

Nazareth wasn't only Jesus' hometown; it was the town that tried to throw him off a cliff. Just north of the fertile Valley of Megiddo, far from rivers, oceans, and major trade routes, it was never the most influential or scenic city in Israel. Perhaps that "off the beaten path" status provided the peace and quiet, tight family bonds, and distance from Roman outposts that many God-fearing Jews preferred during the time of Jesus. Joseph and Mary settled there because Joseph feared Archelaus, the Rome-appointed ruler in Judea (Matt. 2:21–23). Nazareth wasn't prime real estate, but we can imagine its residents were a tightly knit band of survivors on the margins of a Gentile-ridden land.

Settling off the beaten path, Joseph and Mary started a family amid whispers of scandal among their relatives and neighbors who were well aware that Mary was pregnant though only betrothed to Joseph. We can speculate what people thought of Mary's virtue and whether she was excluded from social events and even the day-to-day gatherings in the village. As for Joseph, he may have been either privately or publicly derided by men because he chose to stick with Mary, believing her story about a miraculous conception through the Holy Spirit. Jesus most likely grew up in a strong community, but that can cut both ways when a scandal hits. What might the people of Nazareth have thought of this supposedly illegitimate child?

By the time Jesus launched his public ministry in Nazareth, the synagogue leaders apparently trusted him enough to let him read the Scripture passage one Sabbath and teach on it. However, something was quite different on this particular Sabbath. Jesus wasn't just a carpenter who had moved shop to Capernaum.

Before he stood up to teach on Isaiah 61:1–2, Jesus had already launched his public ministry—healing many, casting out demons, and preaching—but he had only done so *in other towns*. Although Jesus was an itinerant prophet and teacher, he had previously settled in the town of Capernaum, a larger and more strategically located village on the banks of the Sea of Galilee. The Gospels also note that, soon after his return trip to Nazareth, Jesus chose most of his disciples from Capernaum as well. Perhaps Jesus wanted to escape the looks of scorn or just wanted to live next to a beautiful lake.

This move to Capernaum was likely a sore point with the people of Nazareth. Most families built extra rooms on their homes when their children grew up and married. It wasn't exactly common to go away to college and only visit the folks for holidays. By the time Jesus declared that he was about to fulfill the prophecy of Isaiah, there may have already been an intense back story that colored what people thought of him. We may imagine them thinking, "How could an illegitimate runaway carpenter perform miracles and save us as the chosen 'Messiah'?"

We don't have a clear chronology for Jesus' return to Nazareth. Perhaps Jesus performed miracles and then taught in the synagogue. Perhaps he healed people after they heard his talk. Either way, the people of Nazareth heard rumors about the miracles of Jesus, and many were having none of it.

It may be hard for us to imagine what exactly Jesus was declaring about himself in front of an already skeptical audience. Isaiah 61 was linked directly to the restoration of Israel from nearly six hundred years of exile and the coming of God's rule over them. This wasn't just a military victory over Rome; this was a world-changing homecoming for the Jewish people scattered throughout the ancient world. We don't have a grid to understand this kind of weary expectation and fragile hope.

So far as we can tell, Jesus' sermon didn't raise any eyebrows—at first. Everyone spoke well of him. Perhaps it took a little time for the people to process what they had just heard and what he had implied. But the people soon began to question how the son of Joseph, a woodworker, could possibly be a miracle-performing carpenter who would bring the rule of God and the return from exile. We can read this story with a variety of tones and inflections, but based on Jesus' sharp response, it's clear that they were doubtful about him. We could paraphrase it as, "Who does this son of Joseph think he is?" The irony for readers of the Gospels is that Jesus had just been revealed at his baptism as God's chosen instrument for ushering in God's kingdom. The people in his hometown couldn't get past his humble origins, and Luke carefully juxtaposed the two scenes: God's affirmation followed by hometown rejection.

Jesus saw what was happening and pointed out the elephant in the room: their doubt. They would have been familiar with the saying, "Physician, heal yourself," which Jesus used preemptively. This saying was an arrogant assault on Jesus' pretense to speak so highly of himself and his mission for the world. The phrase mocked Jesus' ability to heal: "You say you're a physician, but you're just as sick as the rest of us." They didn't believe that Jesus could repeat the miracles he performed at Capernaum. Maybe they were bitter that he left home. Perhaps they attributed the reports of his miraculous works to rumors and exaggerations. They didn't have newspapers or before-and-after pictures to show about their healings. There were plenty of healing hoaxes back then. While people in Jesus' day were far more open to displays of the divine in daily life than many are today, they could not believe that small-town Jesus was capable of the rumors they'd heard.

Jesus didn't waste any time in confronting the people. He saw the effects of doubt on his audience, and so he cut to the chase with a dire warning: The people of Nazareth were in danger of rejecting God's work in their midst. In fact, God was already moving to save the Gentiles as foreshadowed during the time of Elijah and Elisha.

Jesus made one of the most biting critiques a Jew could make of a fellow Jew. He suggested that God was active among the Gentiles rather than among them. He suggested this by retelling the stories of Elijah (1 Kings 17) and Elisha (2 Kings 5) where a widow in Zarephath and a Syrian army general were both touched by God while the people of God, the Israelites, rejected two of the greatest prophets the Lord ever sent.

With hindsight being 20/20, Elijah and Elisha became archetypes for the ideal prophets in Jesus' time. When Jesus wanted to explain the significance of the ministry of John the Baptist, he compared him to Elijah. And the miracles of Jesus bear a striking resemblance to those performed by Elisha, such as raising a child from the dead. These connections with Elijah and Elisha during the ministry of Jesus were significant clues for the Jewish people, which makes the words of Jesus at Nazareth about God's ministry to Gentiles all the more striking.

By retelling these stories, Jesus was essentially trying to shake his people awake: "Look! God is doing something right in front of you, but you're missing it, just like the Jews at the time of Elijah and Elisha!" Jesus' audience was well aware of how wicked the people of Israel were during the time of Elijah and Elisha. Their stories took place during the reign of Ahab and Jezebel. The Jews who later returned from exile were determined to stay faithful to the Lord. The synagogues existed as a bulwark against repeating the mistakes that occurred during the time of Elijah and Elisha. The story itself was not the problem with Jesus' audience. The problem was his application. Jesus was comparing the people of Nazareth to apostate Israel under the rule of Ahab. To make matters even more controversial, Jesus suggested that God's restoration of Israel from exile would also come to the hated Gentiles—the ones who "caused" this mess in the first place. This was an unthinkable theological statement.

Moreover, that an "ordinary carpenter" would dare to proclaim the end of the exile, compare God-fearing Jews to apostate Israel, and extend God's saving work beyond themselves to the Gentiles was too much for the people of Nazareth. There was no way a supposedly illegitimate child born into the world through a scandalous union could perform miracles, much less lecture them about God abandoning them for the Gentiles. The tension that may have simmered throughout Jesus' childhood and adulthood finally boiled over during his public ministry. Many thought that this delusional carpenter had gone too far, and they wanted to make him pay.

We don't know how many people tried to throw Jesus off the cliff, but Jesus was either strong or clever enough to evade them. This mysterious escape concludes one of the worst family reunions of all time. It must have been a long and reflective journey from Nazareth back to Capernaum.

By the time the people of Nazareth tried to toss Jesus off a cliff, any friction he may have had with his family suddenly paled in comparison. This wasn't just a loss of common ground; this was an attempt to kill an alleged false prophet.

INSIDERS WHO WELCOME OUTSIDERS ARE WELCOME
Where Is God?

The people of Nazareth thought they knew where to find God: in his temple, of course. Jesus exploded the conventional wisdom of his day with two nearly unbelievable claims. For starters, God was among them, ending the exile, healing the broken, and announcing God's favor through the ministry of Jesus. However, God was also present with the Gentiles. God wasn't just for the Jewish people.

I wonder how we would answer this question today: Where is God? Is God in a church building? On a mission trip? At a Christian music concert? At a Christian ministry conference? At a Christian book signing?

A glance at the ministry of Jesus tells us where to find God: among the poor, prisoners, sick, grieving, and Gentiles. This certainly goes against the grain of our thinking today where prosperity and carefree living is often interpreted as a sign of God's favor. Speaking for American Christians, many of us have been taught that material prosperity is a sign of God's blessing and approval. And if those with plenty are the blessed, it doesn't take a lot of imagination to figure out what God thinks of those struggling, living in poverty, or uncertain about their future. We don't explicitly say they're cursed, but we may wonder if they have squandered God's gifts or offended him in some way.

Is God moving among the people we've already ruled out? Is God calling us to bless those who are least like us? There is a tension throughout this story between what people expected God to do and how God actually worked. The people of Nazareth didn't think that a carpenter born amidst a scandal could possibly heal anyone, much less save them as God's anointed Messiah. No one would have been so bold as to suggest that the Messiah would save the Gentiles instead of God's chosen people.

If we're honest with ourselves, we want Jesus to look like us—whether he's wearing a suit and advising business professionals in the board room or dressed in jeans and talking about the Bible over lunch in a cafe. The Messiah didn't show up in a way that connected with the expectations of the people of Nazareth. They couldn't imagine that God would use a humble carpenter. But more than that, they didn't believe God would want to reach out to the Gentiles, the people God had ordered them to stay away from by means of laws and warnings. Jesus associated the presence of God with the wrong people, and that became a huge stumbling block for the people of Nazareth.

It's uncomfortable to admit that God loves the people you've always ruled out. It's frightening to think that God may not be quite so comfortable among us in our pews—perhaps he prefers to work in the places where we'd rather not go. The tension between Jesus and his hometown is rooted in the people of Nazareth wanting God to work among them according to their own categories and expectations where they maintained a measure of control and familiarity.

Can we blame them? Who doesn't want control and familiarity? These very things became the greatest barriers between the people of Nazareth and their ability to follow God's Messiah. Before we pray for God to make our lives more comfortable or to meet us where we are, perhaps we should first ask if God wants to send us to people who make us feel less comfortable or if he's already working someplace where we can join him.

What Can Jesus Do?

When Jesus announced his ministry in Nazareth, he was met with the challenge: "Do here in your hometown what we have heard that you did in Capernaum" (Luke 4:23). There is a sense in which the people would only believe in Jesus once they saw firsthand what he was capable of; and it's likely they would not have believed his miracles even if they had witnessed them. This probably goes back to their resentment over his leaving home and their doubt that Jesus, a mere woodworker, was as great a wonder-worker as the rumors suggested.

If we follow the version of the story as presented by Matthew and Mark, it's hard to escape the possibility that our doubts limit what God will do among us: "He could not do any miracles there, except lay his hands on a few sick people and heal them" (Mark 6:5). While we know that Jesus healed the son of a man who confessed his struggles with unbelief, the people of Nazareth almost completely shut out any possibility of him working miracles among them. This line of thinking is supported by James in his epistle: "But when you ask, you must believe and not doubt, because the one who doubts is like a wave of the sea, blown and tossed by the wind. That person should not expect to receive anything from the Lord. Such a person is double-minded and unstable in all they do" (James 1:6–8). While Jesus only needs faith the size of a mustard seed to work in our lives, there is something about persistent doubt that can snuff out the work of God among us.

It's frightening to think that God acts in accordance with our faith. Nevertheless, this theme emerges time and time again in the Gospels. Frequently in Matthew, Jesus healed people "because of their faith." Of course there are other examples of

God sometimes persistently reaching out to someone who doubted. However, we can't escape the trend in Scripture that God essentially descends to our level—meeting us according to the measure of our faith. If we have a small worldview, then God allows that and works from within it. For example, the Bible has several examples of God speaking to his people through dreams, and there are Christians today who still claim that God speaks to them through their dreams. While it's possible to get carried away with dream interpretation, it is also possible that we limit God's work when we rule out the very things he does over and over again in the Bible. Is it a surprise that people who do not believe that God still speaks through dreams never experience messages from God through dreams and that those open to God speaking through dreams sometimes sense God's prompting through their dreams?

Our minds need renewal, as Paul said in Romans 12:1–2. If we are going to faithfully follow Jesus, then we can't let our culture or those who misunderstand the presence of God to either limit or misconstrue what we believe. The people of Nazareth were only willing to believe what they had seen Jesus do. They refused to believe what they'd heard about him. Are we willing to believe that the story of Scripture can be true for us too? While we shouldn't try to force God's hand or always pray for a miracle or message through a dream, what would it look like to remain open to the supernatural work of God in our lives today?

What Is a Prophet's Job?

The role of prophets throughout the Scriptures was to deliver God's Word to his people, which often meant disrupting the comfortable and complacent. If we read the stories of Jeremiah, Isaiah, and Ezekiel with pictures of eager audiences in our imaginations, we're missing out on the hatred and violence directed at them. One of the themes that runs through the Gospels is the inability of Jesus' audience to recognize the fact that they were repeating the mistakes of previous generations by rejecting God's chosen messenger in their midst (see 2 Chron. 24:19; Neh. 9:26; Ezek. 2:5; Hos. 9:7).

Jesus alluded to this in Nazareth when he compared himself to a prophet who is never welcome in his hometown. Much like Jeremiah, who was tossed in a well by his countrymen, Jesus faced violent opposition when he delivered God's message.

The sands of time have a way of softening the messages of prophets since we're far enough removed from their circumstances. We miss how disturbing their messages were to their original audiences. For example, nowadays Billy Graham is one of the most familiar and widely accepted Christian leaders in the world. However, when he took his evangelism crusades to the South during the segregation era in America, he refused to allow separate seating areas. While Graham wasn't a civil rights advocate like Martin Luther King, Jr., he did stand up for racial unity in the context of his crusades, and he was bitterly opposed because of it by many Christians in his day. Now, fifty years later, Christians can't imagine Billy Graham as a polarizing or controversial figure. However, there certainly was a time when Graham was viewed by many as a dangerous threat to "God's racial order."

We can look back at Jeremiah or Billy Graham and believe they were on the right side. There's no doubt that Israel was rebelling against God and that segregating people according to race is a great evil. However, discerning who the true prophets are today is quite another matter. For many of us, simply hearing someone being referred to as a "modern prophet" prompts us to put up our guard. Anyone who claims to speak for God is met with suspicion since so many have used such a claim to advance their own agendas, bullying and abusing all who would question their God-given messages and, inevitably, authority.

However, there is no doubt that God has used people to share very specific and important messages at particular points in time. These prophets often weren't the kinds of nice people we'd invite over for dinner. They used nudity to demonstrate a coming exile, animal dung as a cooking fuel to demonstrate the coming poverty for Israel, and marriage to a prostitute to illustrate God's love for his people. They made people uncomfortable and challenged them to change their ways and repent of their sins.

The ministry and message of Jesus brought significant discomfort to the people in his hometown. He said just about the last thing his friends, family, and neighbors wanted to hear: "God is coming back. The Gentiles are part of his plan, and you're missing it." Jesus' first sermon back home was far from a popular success. He did not win over any new followers. Attendance, so to speak, was probably way down the next Sabbath.

It's common today to look at numbers as a way of indicating success. Naturally, the most sales indicates the most popular product. However, when it comes to following God, numbers have a way of clouding the bigger picture. Popular support is not necessarily the mark of someone in touch with God. In fact, Mark followed this story in Nazareth with Jesus choosing his small band of disciples, a misfit group of temperamental fishermen, a tax collector, a failed revolutionary, and a mix of other peasants who had no credibility. They didn't watch Jesus grow up. They didn't have the same connections with his family. And yet, they were the ones who ended up believing in and following him.

Perhaps certain groups of Christians think they have an exclusive claim to Jesus today. I spent years thinking that my own denomination best understood and represented Jesus. We spent so much time reading the Bible and praying that we had to be right. Over the years, many other faithful Christians, who think differently about God and church than I do, have helped me change my beliefs about my exclusive claim to God. They've showed sides of Jesus I'd been missing and parts of the Bible I'd overlooked. We all do this.

Our danger is that we may resist those who present a side of Jesus, God, or the Bible that makes us uncomfortable instead of prayerfully considering what they have to say. Could we be wrong? Could Jesus be a little different from what we imagine? Have we reshaped God into our own image to the point that we miss the radical message of Jesus? While we have to be careful about jumping on cultural trends or teachings that pull us away from the centrality of Jesus for our faith, there is every reason to expect that our notions about faithfully following Jesus may shift and evolve from time to time. The people who were the most firm and unbending in their theology were the ones who missed Jesus when he challenged their notions about God and Gentiles. It is always good to remember that it wasn't those who humbly repented and reoriented their thinking around his words of truth with whom Jesus clashed; it was those who boasted an exclusive claim on God.

OUR LEAP OF FAITH

We can still go to the cliff in Nazareth today. We can wonder who in their right mind would try to kill someone there, much less kill God incarnate. We may shake our heads at how the people of Nazareth rejected Jesus in their midst. However, I'm not at all confident in my own fail-proof ability to recognize the work and presence of God in my midst today. Jesus said that when we do something for the least of these, we do it for him. Honestly, when I see the "least of these," my first impulse many times has been to turn away. Seeing Jesus in others has required rethinking my schedule, priorities, and perception of people. Just as God wanted to use a simple carpenter and a band of fishermen and misfits to proclaim the coming of his world-changing kingdom, he wants his people today to see him at work among those regarded by our culture as scandalous, useless, or broken beyond repair.

If someone showed up at our churches and declared that God had chosen to reveal himself among the unemployed, homeless, institutionally sick, imprisoned, and impoverished, I wonder what we'd do. Would we shake our heads? Would we walk out? Would we repent? Or would we start looking for a high enough cliff?

NOTE

1. "Esther John," Westminster Abbey, accessed April 15, 2013, http://www.westminster-abbey.org/our-history/people/esther-john.

▮3 THE PHARISEES

A MESSIAH WHO KEEPS THE RIGHT COMPANY

Hudson Taylor, the founder of the China Inland Mission, is rarely thought of as controversial or provocative today. His contemporaries would have disagreed. As a missionary to China, Taylor brought much-needed medical supplies, prompted hundreds of missionaries to serve overseas, and reached thousands with the gospel. It's hard to argue with a man who leaves the comforts of home to serve and preach to others. However, arguing is exactly what happened when Taylor and the men and women on his mission team started to dress like the Chinese.

Taylor's travels throughout China took place from 1854 to 1905, and while missionaries possessed many commendable qualities back then, British missionaries such as Taylor lived in a colonial context where the gospel and Western culture had been so linked together that the two were not recognized as distinct from one another. For example, missionaries would go to China to preach, but it was unthinkable to actually live like the Chinese, let alone live among them. Chinese converts were expected to imitate the cultural and religious practices of the British missionaries. Missionaries also had the benefit of protection by the most powerful army and navy in the world—a fall-back option if their audience turned against them, as happened at times in China.

Taylor refused all protection from the British armed forces and mandated that everyone in the China Inland Mission dress like the local Chinese with the intention of living among them. Taylor fought against the tide in the missions movement, and criticism followed. Besides tossing aside the supposedly superior British culture, Taylor raised more than a few eyebrows at tea time by encouraging the female missionaries to adopt Chinese dress. Not only that, but Taylor also broke new missionary ground by appointing laypersons as missionaries rather than clergy, requiring missionaries to raise all their financial support, accepting single women alongside men, and basing his headquarters in Asia rather than in Europe.

Could a Christian ever do such a thing?

The methods of Taylor are not controversial at all today, but his Chinese dress code (among other things) broke boundaries in the late 1800s. Missionaries were allowed to get close to the Chinese people without actually having to become one of them. For many British missionaries at the time, Taylor was the wrong kind of missionary. In many cases in the 1800s, missionaries were expected to get close but not too close to the people among whom they ministered. Of course, any willing converts who responded to the gospel and crossed over to the British missionaries in both religion and culture were welcomed with open arms. Ironically, both the Chinese people and the British missionaries Taylor challenged needed a dose of the freedom that the gospel brings. It's fascinating to look at what happens when someone comes along to disrupt these boundaries between "sinner" and "saint" to bring salvation to both sides. That disruption is exactly what Jesus brought in many situations in the Gospels.

WRONG PEOPLE, WRONG MESSIAH

As mentioned before, at the time of Jesus there was no unified view of what the Messiah was supposed to do. At the same time, observant Jews did assume that the Messiah would follow the law and keep it perfectly—that is, follow the law as *they* interpreted it. Implied in this would be avoiding any hint of sin or scandal by avoiding Gentiles, the ritually impure (such as lepers), and those who led sexually immoral lives. In addition, any pure and patriotic Jew would have shunned tax collectors, who exploited their countrymen in the service of the occupying Roman army and puppet government. The story of the Pharisee and the tax collector who went to the temple to pray tells us most of what we need to know about the mind-set of the religious leaders at the time of Jesus. While a tax collector cringed from far off and confessed his sins, the self-righteous Pharisee didn't think twice about cataloguing his many holy accomplishments before God. The Pharisee would never have thought to approach the tax collector to heal him or help him change his ways. The Pharisees, who were most zealous for the Jewish Law at Jesus' time, saw sin as a one-way transaction where contamination would be the only possible result of an encounter with it. Jesus turned this type of thinking on its head by becoming a doctor to those who were sick with sin so that he could heal them. Where the Pharisees saw an opportunity for falling away, Jesus saw a calling to heal and restore.

On one occasion, Jesus, in characteristic fashion, was feasting with known sinners and despised tax-collectors. As the Pharisees observed this, they were scandalized. We can paraphrase the Pharisees' statement to Jesus' disciples: "How dare your rabbi have fellowship with known lawbreakers and criminals rather than with upstanding and righteous people like ourselves?" Jesus' reply to the Pharisees' pointed question was unequivocal: "Healthy people don't need a doctor—sick people do" (Matt. 9:12 NLT). As we read in the gospels of Matthew and John, Jesus dined with the wicked and enjoyed himself at parties and festivals. He did all the wrong things, chief of which was being seen with the wrong people.

Imagine you've dedicated your entire life to perfectly following the law of God. You've avoided any trace of sin, including the people who could lead you to sin. In fact, it's hard to find anyone who has been more loyal and faithful as a follower of God, since you've studied under the best law teachers in your country. They are wise and measured, helping you navigate what it means to obey God. They offer parameters that explain the complexities of God's law, and after studying them for years, you're certain that you're on the right course.

What would you make of a simple, uneducated preacher who showed up in your village and suggested that much of your thinking was wrong or at least significantly misguided?

This man has never studied under your tutors. There's no chance he could understand the law of God better or offer a superior way to obey the truth of God. This preacher, prophet, or fraud, whatever he really is, can't be from God. He doesn't even know the most basic thing about remaining pure and holy: He parties with tax collectors—those horrible traitors who bow before Rome and cheat God and God's people. Doesn't he realize that these people will pollute him and make him unclean before a holy God?

It wouldn't take a religious scholar to recognize that such a person was clearly unfit to speak on behalf of God.

The religion scholars at the time of Jesus had examples of God making the unclean pure through sacrifice. They knew what God *could* do. Somehow they became so entangled in trying to remain pure, to be perfect before a holy God, that they forgot how far God is willing to go to redeem broken people.

When Jesus partied with Matthew and his fellow tax collectors, he was extending something radical to them. He was accepting them by eating with them. This wasn't just a dinner party. This was entering into their social circles—a gesture we don't quite have an equivalent for today. This was also the most certain way for a Jewish rabbi to discredit his ministry before the more observant Jews. Jesus wasn't inviting Matthew and his friends over for dinner; they were inviting him to join them on their turf. And he accepted their invitation with no reservations. Jesus didn't arrive at Matthew's house with a list of doctrines he and his guests must accept or a list of behaviors they needed to practice to have the Messiah over for dinner. Jesus started with Matthew and his friends right where they were: intrigued by Jesus but not holy or pure by any means.

When the Pharisees singled out "sinners" in addition to tax collectors, this meant that Jesus was eating among notorious law-breakers who did not follow dietary restrictions, purity rules, or observe the Sabbath. Perhaps it was a job that kept them unclean, such as a tanner, prostitute, or tax collector. Or perhaps they didn't follow the law because they didn't see the need to do so. Besides the political stigma of collaborating with the enemy and cheating their countrymen, tax collectors were also considered ritually unclean because they associated and fellowshiped with Gentiles. Instead of challenging them on their corrupt lifestyles, Jesus joined them for a party. Rather than warning them about the wrath of God and judgment for their sins, Jesus joined them around a table for a conversation. The reaction of the Pharisees tells us that Jesus wasn't saying enough to meet their approval. They could not believe that Jesus wasn't criticizing these corrupt thieves.

Perhaps we can place ourselves in their shoes and understand the Pharisees' perspective. Would we want to risk giving a corrupt person the wrong idea that we approve of their actions? We can see that the Pharisees in this scene had boiled down holy living to outward appearances, and it's quite likely that we do the same thing today. There is a certain look that we expect for a clean-cut, modest Christian versus a "backsliding" Christian.

When Jesus responded to their criticism, he made a striking departure from their expectations for a messiah. Instead of taking on the mantle of a pure spiritual and military leader who would cleanse the land, which was one view of the Messiah at that time, Jesus designated himself as a doctor sent to heal sick people.

Jesus summarized this role as a healing doctor well when he quoted the saying from Hosea: "I desire mercy, not sacrifice" (see Matt. 9:13; Hos. 6:6). The Pharisees expected someone who was a ritualist, that is, one who majored in the jots and tittles of the Torah. Therefore, the passage from Hosea must have been just as disturbing as it was humiliating for the Pharisees to hear. Hosea, the well-known prophet whom God ordered to marry a prostitute, represents the daring love of God on display in Jesus who defies common wisdom and overrules custom. Perhaps the reference to Hosea particularly struck a chord if prostitutes or notoriously immoral women had been among Matthew's dinner guests. The Pharisees, by contrast, seemed to be expecting a Messiah who was more like the prophet Jonah who would rather sail across the world than be in the presence of the spiritually sick.

By quoting this passage from Hosea, Jesus also picked up on another theme from the prophets that shows up frequently in the Gospels: the prophets' critique of the temple and observance of the law. Ever since God gave the law to Moses, there had been a tension between wholehearted devotion to God—a devotion that could be expressed by observing the law—and merely going through the motions of the law. In Isaiah, the Lord laments, "These people come near to me with their mouth and honor me with their lips, but their hearts are far from me. Their worship of me is based on merely human rules they have been taught" (29:13). The tone of the prophets toward the temple and observance of the law grew so sharp at times that some scholars have even suggested that there were pro- and anti-temple factions during the time of the prophets. While it's more likely that the prophets were criticizing Judaism from within rather than dividing it, we can see how Jesus picked up where these prophets left off.

As the Pharisees mastered the theological science of excluding sinners, keeping the law as technical as possible and observing all of the mandated sacrifices for the temple, they lost sight of the reason why God gave them the law and the sacrificial system in the first place. What the Pharisees had turned into a system of punishment and exclusion, Jesus refocused on healing, restoration, and inclusion. God declared to the people of Israel, "If my people, who are called by my name, will humble themselves and pray and seek my face and turn from their wicked ways, then I will hear from heaven, and I will forgive their sin and will heal their land" (2 Chron. 7:14). The purpose of the law was for healing and restoration, and Jesus lived out that truth by seeking out the "wrong people" and meeting them where they were, even if that meant associating with the worst sinners.

Not So Fast

The conversation between Jesus and the disciples of John the Baptist, a story immediately following the confrontation at Matthew's home, further exposes the tension between Jesus and the religious leaders of his day. The religious leaders had made fasting an essential requirement for holy living, when in reality, it was only required during the Day of Atonement. In other words, they were judging Jesus based not on the law (since we suppose that Jesus would have fasted during the Day of Atonement) but on the oral tradition that prescribed fasting twice a week (see Luke 18:12). In contrast to this austerity, Jesus spent his time partying with sinners and never publicly displayed any outward indication that he was fasting.

Why didn't Jesus make a point of showing his religious commitment to God by fasting? While Jesus certainly did fast, he made a point of keeping it a secret. Most of the things he did publicly damaged his reputation, such as his meal with Matthew. Even when met with the accusation that his disciples didn't fast, Jesus never took the time to debate the point.

We can see just how dramatically he didn't care about their perception of him. Instead, Jesus pointed them to the reasons why someone is supposed to fast. Presumably, someone fasts to draw near to God. However, if God is at a party, then fasting outside of the party is defeating its purpose. When God is "far away," then fasting as a means of withdrawing from the needs and concerns of this world can prove a helpful way to focus our minds on God. However, Jesus stripped away any outward implications that may have been attached to the practice of fasting in his day: Fasting does not mark someone as truly religious. Fasting is not a badge. It is a means to an end—meeting God.

As Jesus deconstructed the way John's disciples viewed fasting, he also warned them that major changes were coming to their conceptions of meeting with God. As if to call attention to their austerity, he spoke in terms of patching old clothes and reusing old wineskins—both of which fail. A worn-out shirt will continue to fall apart with a new patch on it, and a used-up wineskin has already expanded from the fermented grape juice. Both must be replaced to accomplish their purposes. Many different interpreters have applied the new wine and wineskins imagery to anything from church meeting formats to changes in theology. Taken in the immediate context, Jesus was speaking of a dramatic shift in how to approach God. Whereas fasting had kept the people of God together for a period of time, Jesus brought a new reality of God among them. They needed to be willing to rethink their practices with God incarnate in their midst. Their practices that had helped them understand or "contain" their knowledge of God needed to be overhauled to hold the new revelation that Jesus brought. If they couldn't accept a messiah who partied with sinners rather than fasting with saints, then perhaps the problem wasn't with the Messiah but with the standards being used to judge the Messiah.

It's difficult to know how far to take the words of Jesus. While we should temper his statement here by reading it alongside his prediction that there will be fasting when he is taken away from them, there is no denying that the old religious order had shifted dramatically with his arrival. There is a new intimacy with God because of him. The Holy Spirit would soon fulfill God's promise to write his law on our hearts. Jesus was in the process of adopting us as sons and daughters with a full inheritance. There is still much to celebrate today, even as fasting remains an appropriate way to seek the Lord.

The great irony of this exchange with John's disciples is their willingness to earnestly fast and deny themselves comfort even though the God to whom they were praying and for whom they were fasting stood in their midst, inviting them to celebrate with him. When God invites you to celebrate, ignoring God's freedom while fasting instead becomes just as much an act of disobedience as any other sin that elevates our own wisdom over God's. Even with God in their midst, the disciples of John the Baptist may have discovered that they liked the "status" they gained as fasting, holy men. It gave them a religious identity that set them apart and made them unique. What could these holy men gain by reaching out to the notorious sinners of their day?

We would never suggest that anyone who fasts or lives simply is merely grandstanding. However, we can make a false assumption that God demands austerity from us. While fasting, being simplistic, and keeping certain company may help someone follow God better, they don't automatically draw us closer to God or create boundaries between insiders and outsiders. We can see that the Pharisees and the disciples of John the Baptist had a checklist for holy living, and Jesus intentionally lived in such a way that he may as well have torn it up in front of them.

We can imagine that Jesus wasn't telling his followers to party all of the time. In fact, he told his followers that there would come a time when they would fast, and he told them to pray in secret. Jesus set out to destroy boundaries and categories based on external behavior and personal effort. If the religious trend of the day was to always feast and party, maybe Jesus would have shown up fasting just to drive home his bigger point that God's life is freely available to all who are thirsty.

The disciples of John wanted to know why Jesus didn't fast and tithe like them. Jesus wanted to know why they weren't thirsty and willing to join him at the table.

Game Over

As it turned out, the disciples of John weren't the only ones who struggled to believe Jesus was the Messiah. As we discussed in the first chapter, John himself struggled to believe. Prompted by the doubts of John the Baptist, several of John's disciples relayed John's question to Jesus. John wasn't the kind of guy to beat around the bush. "Are you the one who is to come, or should we expect someone else?" (Matt. 11:3). Jesus pointed to his actions as proof of his identity, implying that he was the Messiah but being careful not to say things too explicitly, so that he would not be arrested by the authorities before fulfilling his mission. But after the disciples of John left, Jesus offered a defense of John's ministry and his own. After praising John and aligning his ministry with Elijah's, Jesus offered a stinging rebuke of his generation for being childlike in their religious devotion.

The religious practices of this generation had become a kind of game where the holy insiders made up the rules and freely banned anyone they saw fit. Their childlike rules lacked consistency and only resembled true devotion to God in the way that children playing in a marketplace imitated a funeral or wedding with "play" mourning or dancing. Whether Jesus feasted or John fasted, this generation always found a loophole to dismiss Jesus or John and to maintain their own position and lifestyle. They had cut themselves off from God with their overly pious rules and standards, and the coming of Jesus and John merely exposed them. If Jesus avoided feasting with sinners, they would have found another way to dismiss him, just as they had dismissed John's ministry in the wilderness.

Ironically, for all of these accusations of being childish about holy living, Jesus suggested that the answer is still found in being like a child. The difference is that we are all called to be childlike, not childish. The "wise" will develop complex explanations and systems of thinking that may cloud the simplicity of a God who says, "Come to my table and find rest!" Those who become like little children and are willing to accept God (see Matt. 11:25) will be given true wisdom that plays out in the way they live. However, the wise and learned may resist the simplicity of God and resort to childish foolishness. We are all destined to become like children, but the only way to find God is by becoming more childlike first.

Feasting at Cana

If we take the writings of John as bookends for the life of Jesus, we find that wedding feasts mark the beginning of Jesus' ministry and the beginning of his visible reign on earth. While it's easy to get lost in speculation over the confrontation between Jesus and his mother during the wedding feast of Cana, let's take a step back and look at what Jesus' new disciples would have made of this situation. They had just been fasting and praying in the desert with John, confessing their sins and waiting for the Messiah. We can only imagine their elation when John pointed out Jesus. Perhaps that excitement dried up during the wedding feast in Cana.

There is no record of Jesus' reason for attending this feast. If anything, it reminds us that Jesus lived as an involved member of his community. In fact, the comparison between Jesus and John the Baptist could not be more striking. Perhaps Jesus' new disciples feared they were wasting their time with this wedding feast. Weren't they doing something for God out in the wilderness? Why would the Messiah waste his time on a wedding feast when there were Romans to expel from the land? There were miracles to perform.

Jesus would have agreed with that last line to a certain extent. There indeed were miracles to perform, and he shared his first public miracle at this wedding feast. He needed to make a lot of wine— two hundred gallons of the finest wine to be precise. While the disciples were no doubt elated to see the power of Jesus on display, what good would an abundance of wine do? You can't expect to drink the whole Roman army under the table. Perhaps they saw this miracle as a waste of power. Or perhaps they took comfort in seeing something genuinely miraculous. What we can know for sure is this: They weren't thinking the same thing as Jesus.

As Jesus turned the water jugs formerly used for ceremonial washing into wine jugs, he made a powerful statement about what God wanted from his people. Rather than commanding them to stay away and wash their sins, they were invited to draw near and to celebrate. Without the ceremonial washing jugs, God's people could still confess their sins, but the outward rituals lost their significance. There was no time to wash. They had the best wine to enjoy.

With all of the parties that Jesus attended throughout the Gospels, we can see that the wedding feast at Cana set up a pattern. This was no exception or one-time splurge. Jesus routinely met people where they were rather than hiding in the desert — that is, until he became too popular and controversial to enter a town. The thing about a party is that anyone can attend. By its very design, a party is inclusive. There are plenty of reasons why someone wouldn't go to the temple in Jesus' day or attend church in our own time. That's why God's kingdom celebration is such good news. Anyone can come to the party in God's kingdom. To the surprise of Jesus' contemporaries, it worked.

WHO ARE THE WRONG PEOPLE TODAY?
What Is a Kingdom Party?

Many associate spirituality with fasting and austere living. And while there is great freedom in simplicity, Jesus challenged our notions of holy living with his regular attendance at parties — even parties with disreputable hosts and guests. In fact, he risked his reputation by partying with all of the "wrong" people. That may seem like a frivolous oversight on the part of Jesus. He lost popular support from the religious establishment to share a meal with notorious sinners. This is an example of the insider/outsider tension throughout the New Testament as God reached out to both the notorious sinners and to Gentiles outside of Israel.

We experience the same tensions today. One friend of mine plays in a band that performs at weddings and also serves as part of her church's worship team. Sometimes they play in local bars as a way to promote their band. They have great conversations with people who would never visit a church. Unfortunately, some folks at my friend's church see these bar gigs as a problem because they're hanging out with the wrong people.

How will someone who hangs out at a bar each night learn about God if Christians treat them like a toxic disease? This tension comes up over and over again as Christians model the way Jesus reached out to the "wrong" people and then their commitment to Christ is called into question.

How could a Christian lead a Bible study in a bar? How could a Christian reach out to those who support abortion or gay rights? How could a Christian visit prison inmates who knowingly harmed others? These are tough, divisive questions. I've even asked one or two of them myself at one point or another in the past. It's much easier to manage appearances when it comes to sin. Keeping a clean veneer is much easier than asking God to search our hearts and to make us pure. Keeping our distance from the mess of others keeps life simple and never threatens our reputations. In that case, we would never have to deal with someone questioning our motives or risking the loss of positions or relationships.

What Is the Mark of a Follower of Jesus?

I used to think that the mark of a strong Christian was daily Bible reading of at least fifteen or thirty minutes. If that person took notes in a journal and highlighted the Bible, he or she was probably going to become a missionary or pastor.

We're always looking for external markers of religious devotion that set apart insiders and outsiders. It's a natural tendency among people who are always looking to define themselves against other people. There are the real chefs who don't cook with salted butter, sports fans who wear certain jerseys, and the environmentally conscious who buy organic vegetables and biodegradable laundry soap. Among Christians today, we may create boundaries based on which movies people watch, how they dress, how often they go to church, how often they read their Bibles, or which political party they support. Even hot-button issues today function more as tools for division. Homosexuality is certainly a difficult topic for biblical interpretation, but its inflated importance among Christians today is largely a function of religious leaders using it as a divider between sinners and saints. If there's one group that does not feel welcome in evangelical churches today, it's homosexuals, since they have been labeled as "notorious sinners." Consequently, if we are taking these stories about Jesus seriously, we should expect that the followers of Jesus would be invited to party with homosexuals. Keep in mind, Jesus was invited to feast with "notorious sinners" who were despised by the religious leaders of his day. While Jesus did not encourage the tax collectors to keep cheating or unfaithful women to leave their husbands, he didn't turn down an opportunity to meet them where they were.

The mark of a committed follower of Jesus may be a willingness to share the love of God among the wrong people rather than practicing the right theology among the holy. If I'm not willing to risk my reputation to let a "notorious sinner" know about God's love, then I may need some healing too.

While there are plenty of ways we can get theology and religious devotion wrong, that doesn't mean we shouldn't pursue either of them. I still read my Bible, but I don't look at it as the thing that defines me as a follower of Jesus. The key is that these practices help us keep in touch with God rather than marking us as true Christians. Jesus regularly withdrew to quiet places to pray. He even spent entire nights in prayer. The ways Jesus taught with authority from the Scriptures suggest that he'd devoted a significant amount of time to study and reflection. Whether you fast, pray the daily hours, study the Bible, or practice silence before God, each can usher you into his presence and draw you near to him. These practices are not our measures for one another. They help us create a space to meet with God.

How Do We Respond to Criticism?

Any time we deal with faith and religious beliefs, we're going to bump into strong beliefs, assumptions, and major life decisions and commitments. Hanging out with the wrong people may result in criticism and even expulsion from certain religious groups. We can see that while Jesus received criticism for hanging out with the wrong people, he wasn't above offering a sharp response. This leads to a fine line where we have to balance the teachings of Jesus to love one another, even our enemies, but also respond to critics with honesty and accuracy.

As we see Jesus' frustration with the Pharisees for their criticism of his ministry and of John the Baptist, he finally called them out for their childish demands. In their eyes, no one was doing religion right except for them. Jesus exposed their unreasonable mind-set with a critique of his own. This was not a mild-mannered statement or lighthearted quip. Jesus called powerful religious leaders "childish." Perhaps it's hard to see how Jesus could be so kind and forgiving to sinners who repented while reserving harsh statements for religious leaders.

Whether or not we have a clear sense of how to respond to criticism, receiving criticism, even from a relative stranger, can be quite hard to take. If you've been part of a church or joined an online conversation about Christianity, you most likely know the sting of criticism and judgment. Responding with wisdom is never easy when we feel attacked and devalued. If anything, we want to strike back to prove our own self-worth in an attempt to reclaim our dignity.

As Jesus spent time with notorious sinners and his reputation suffered among the religious leaders and John the Baptist's disciples, he managed to keep a clear perspective of whose opinion mattered. In fact, he didn't even mention the fact that he fasted regularly. He didn't do it in public like them. He cared so little about their opinion of him that he called out their own hypocrisy without justifying himself. This line between exposing faulty logic without trying to defend oneself is a tough one to walk. Our affirmation and worth comes only from God, and it's easy to lose sight of that when criticism comes from our peers. If anything, the sting of that criticism reminds us how hard it is to rest fully in the love and acceptance of God.

Childlike Faith vs. Childish Thinking

There are days when I fear that I have become too wise for my own good—one of my closest friends even told me this recently. Like many other Christians today, I have committed myself to Bible study and have read my share of theology books. I like to think of myself as learned and, at least in certain circumstances, wise. Because of my education, I have no trouble stepping in to lead a Bible study or to preach a sermon. However, I wonder if this education can sometimes become a liability.

It's not uncommon for me to become skeptical of someone with a very simple faith who depends significantly upon God. While there is a real danger in believing that God orders "everything" toward a specific purpose—the kind of doctrine that manufactures plenty of atheists—I also wonder if I'm too quick to dismiss someone with a simple, childlike faith. I can construct my own rules for who's in and who's out with God—or at least for who's right and who's wrong about theology. Perhaps the wise and learned cynics of today could use a dose of simple, childlike faith.

A HOSPITAL OR A FORTRESS?

Jesus was the Messiah who came to treat those who were sick and, in fact, some who were actually dead. To heal these patients, he had to get to know them on their own terms. This is the reason Jesus was known as a glutton. It wasn't so much that he loved to party, drink, or feast, but that he loved people—especially people who were sick. He wasn't guarding a spiritual fortress. He was setting up a hospital where all were welcome. One of the central marks of Jesus' ministry was his love for people who were spiritually ill and in need of a spiritual cure. The consequences of this vocation were that Jesus had to maintain fellowship with the "wrong" people, or at least wrong in the eyes of others. Rather than spending his time with those who believed themselves to be well, Jesus sought out those who were humble enough to realize their spiritual sickness.

Choosing to stay in a place of comfort where we never have to reach out or risk something is understandable but untenable for a follower of Jesus. The words of Paul come to mind, "If we are 'out of our mind,' as some say, it is for God; if we are in our right mind, it is for you. For Christ's love compels us" (2 Cor. 5:13–14). Those who have been loved much will be empowered to share it freely with others, even if it risks reputation or relationships. Love makes us willing to become all things to all people in the hope of saving some. Love prompts us to travel around the world to tell people about the love and acceptance of God. Love sends us out of our homes to love our neighbors and to heal those who are sick with sin, regardless of what that "sin" might be and regardless of how we might appear to those judging from the outside.

■4 THE GALILEANS

A MESSIAH WHO MAKES SENSE

Life in ancient Rome before and after the birth of Christ was rife with misery and suffering, unless you were among the wealthy elite. The majority of the people in the city perhaps had more in common with refugees or those living in today's impoverished city neighborhoods than with opportunistic young people and educated professionals pursuing career advancement, cultural activities, and a thriving nightlife. As the wealthy consolidated their hold on the land surrounding Rome, the poorest farmers fled to the city in search of work. Instead, they found poverty, inflated grain prices, and a political system that became increasingly centralized and unconcerned with the will of the people.

Without work or food, the poor in the city of Rome became restless. Rebellions had already occurred in a number of Rome's exploited provinces. Politicians soon realized they needed to hold the people at bay without disrupting the status quo. Grain had always been a significant concern among Rome's political leaders. The typical person's diet likely consisted of more than 50 percent bread, since grain was easy to ship and store. But the areas surrounding Rome only produced a fraction of the grain required to feed the people. As a result, most of the grain sold in Rome at a premium had been imported from other parts of modern-day Italy and especially Egypt. Rome's leaders eventually decided it was better to absorb the cost of the grain and give it away than to risk a rebellion. This political strategy relied on either free or significantly discounted grain to help the people eke out a living. Some emperors even handed out loaves of bread to their starving subjects.

The leaders "solved" the problem of widespread unemployment by providing games and other public entertainment events at no cost to the general public. Anything from the gladiator games to circus festivities offered the escape necessary to redirect the attention of the people away from the absolute power of their leaders and to mask the inequity of the economic system that marginalized them. With enough bread to prevent starvation and enough games to divert revolutionary scheming, the Roman leaders managed to "serve" the people just enough to maintain the *Pax Romana* (Roman peace).

The bread supply met a basic human need, but it also provided the best diversion for political leaders who understood that a small concession would go a long way in maintaining their rule. With bread playing such an important role in sustaining life around the time of Christ, we know that the one who controlled the bread supply controlled the masses. Just as the Roman government understood that the financial sacrifice of providing bread ensured their power, the Galileans listening to Jesus—just another group of Roman subjects—saw his bread-multiplying miracle as a definitive sign that he had the traits necessary to become their new king. Jesus knew what they were thinking, and he unexpectedly resisted their plans.

For the Galilean people in the crowds, it perhaps made sense for a messiah to display power such as multiplying loaves of bread, but it didn't make any sense for him to follow that miracle by running off to a mountain to pray all night. It also didn't make sense for Jesus to follow up such a spectacular miracle with incomprehensible teachings about eating his body and drinking his blood. Why would Jesus raise the hopes of the people and then confuse them so dramatically? Why didn't he clarify himself when disciples began to leave? Everyone knew that a king who could multiply loaves of bread had unlimited potential. Why did Jesus "squander" this perfect opportunity?

WRONG BREAD, WRONG MESSIAH

Rising Expectations

As Jesus began to teach the people alongside a mountain, expectations were buzzing throughout Galilee about the authority and power this new teacher wielded. Jesus had performed many miracles, healing the sick and casting out demons. His popularity had grown to the point that more than five thousand men, not including thousands of women and children, had come out to see him. Entering a town to teach or to minister no longer worked with crowds of this size. (And it's also likely that Jesus intentionally taught outside of large towns to avoid the eyes of regional leaders.)

A crowd this size suggests that people weren't just curious about Jesus. His movement had powerful momentum, and he had captured the imaginations of those in the crowd. In ancient Israel, the typical farmer or laborer didn't have personal or sick days to use at his or her discretion. Besides the Sabbath day with its restrictions on travel, work, and holy festivals, there were few breaks for Jews. When people traveled to hear Jesus, they were leaving their work behind—perhaps for several days—putting themselves in financial jeopardy. This was far from calling in "sick" to work. With so many farmers and laborers living near poverty and under heavy taxation from Rome, this was a calculated risk taken only with a reasonable certainty that Jesus could do what the rumors circulating around the villages suggested.

In his account of this miracle and the teachings of Jesus that follow, John noted that the Passover was looming in the background. While no one in the story spelled it out, there were clear implications that a celebration of God's deliverance from slavery in Egypt had been linked with the hope of a coming Messiah. Much like God's mighty defeat of the Egyptians thousands of years before, many believed the Messiah would drive out the Romans and restore the nation of Israel to peace, prosperity, and justice.

The exodus themes shine through in multiple ways in this story, and we can assume that Jesus intentionally incorporated elements of the Passover feast and the story of the Jewish exodus out of Egypt into his teaching at this time. Seeing there was no bread for the people, Jesus singled out Philip for his question in John 6:5. While he singled out Philip, because he was from Bethsaida and therefore the one most familiar with that geographic area, Jesus was also calling to mind God's question for Moses in the desert (see Num. 11:13). In both cases, Jesus in John's gospel and God in the book of Numbers weren't expecting answers. While Philip no doubt panicked, Jesus had a plan in mind. His question merely tested Philip, providing an opportunity for Philip to trust him. At the same time, the people in the crowds were about to be tested in a different way.

The large crowd needed a sign to let them know that the rumors they'd heard were true. They needed their own proof that Jesus would be their Messiah and king. Initially it seemed that Jesus provided exactly the sign that they were looking for. But unfortunately for them, their understanding of it was quite different from what Jesus had intended.

While the people were looking for a reason to confirm Jesus as their Messiah, the prophet like Moses who had been promised to them (Deut. 18:15–19), Jesus took a different view of his miracle. First of all, Jesus performed the miracle out of a genuine compassion for the people. Like a true shepherd, he cared for those entrusted to him. Second, he wanted to teach the people about depending on God and seeking the "food" of God that does not spoil. The multiplied bread wasn't the point. It acted as a signpost pointing the people toward Jesus' heavenly origins and the life that comes from God.

The people could only view Jesus in comparison to Moses and in relation to their daily problems and concerns. They couldn't see beyond these things to the greater truths of God for them. In fact, they were stuck trying to determine whether they should essentially switch their allegiance from Moses to the supposed Messiah. When Jesus replicated the miracle of Moses by feeding the people with bread in the wilderness, that was enough for them. They were far enough away from a town that everyone knew it had to be a miracle. No one could have secretly carried loaves of bread to their location. From their perspective, the miracle met a daily need and indicated that they may never have to work again. With a Messiah providing for them, they would have their needs met, and the Romans would finally get what they deserved. The people then declared triumphantly, "Surely this is the Prophet who is to come into the world" before Jesus and attempting "to come and make him [their] king by force" (John 6:14–15).

But these hopes were dashed to pieces when Jesus fled up the mountain alone. In the first-century world, people did not go mountain climbing or pray on a mountain in search of a "mountaintop" experience. Mountains were generally viewed as rugged, wild, demon-inhabited areas where ordinary people did not gather or go. The fact that Jesus went there alone signaled something strange about him to the dispersed crowds. Normal people would never go alone into the mountains! It's possible that Jesus dispersed the crowd and the disciples because he did not want so many thousands of people to incite a rebellion against Herod Antipas, who was the ruler of that part of the eastern side of the Sea of Galilee. It's also quite likely that Jesus' journey up a mountain hinted that a prophet like Moses, who had also ascended a mountain thousands of years earlier to meet with God, was indeed among them, but that prophet would not lead them in the way they expected.

That Jesus went up to the mountain alone — without the disciples — indicates that the disciples also believed that Jesus should be their king. In other words, they probably sided with the Galileans and did not understand why Jesus would not be the Messiah they desired. Jesus left his disciples and their sky-high expectations to pray for strength. Even his closest disciples were probably whispering complaints, though they were not as aggressive as the crowd.

This Isn't a Sinking Ship

Tucked in between the miracle of the loaves and fishes and the teaching about the bread that came down from heaven, Jesus performed a miracle solely for his disciples. It's likely that they were disappointed to see Jesus so close to being declared king, only for him to run away from it. They were part of his inner circle, and they certainly saw thrones, power, and glory in their future as the servants of Jesus the king. Throughout the Gospels, the disciples argue among themselves about who will be the greatest and who will sit by Jesus' right hand. As they fought against the wind and the waves in their tattered boat in the middle of the night, we can suspect that they felt many things weren't working out as they'd hoped.

In the midst of this discouragement and frustration, Jesus walked to them on the water. We can see yet another parallel with Moses here. While Jesus fed the people bread in the wilderness and met with God on a mountain, he surpassed Moses by walking across the water. Although God parted the waters for Moses, Jesus walked across the water on his own. If his disciples had any doubts about him, Jesus provided a clear sign to encourage them.

As if to drive home his inherent authority, Jesus said, "It is I" (John 6:20) to his disciples as he walked toward them. This is possibly a reference to Exodus 3:14, which could imply Jesus' association with God. Without specifically saying who he was, Jesus alluded to his heavenly origins to his disciples, even though he wasn't what they expected.

Who or What Is the Bread of Life?

The conflict between Jesus and the people of Galilee reached a climax with his "hard teaching" (John 6:60) about eating his body and drinking his blood. However, this lengthy discussion with Jesus about his body and blood isn't the only puzzling part of this exchange. Jesus also spoke about his relationship with the Father, the role of the Father in calling people to himself, and the role of Jesus as protector of all who come to him. This is the advanced course in the Messiah, and the people simply weren't ready for it.

It's possible that Jesus determined that any people willing to forcibly crown him as their king needed the full story about his identity and role. In a moment where the people were about to take control of Jesus' destiny, he revealed some of the most complex aspects of his teaching. In John 4, Jesus had already revealed that he could provide living water that could quench thirst forever. Here he makes the far more shocking claim that his body and blood are food and drink that impart eternal life.

As we discuss the meaning of Jesus' challenging words here about eating and drinking his body and blood and how this correlates with the Lord's Supper in Christian churches today, we dare not oversimplify the complexity of Jesus' discourse. The centuries-old historical debate surrounding the meaning of the Lord's Supper is a hotly debated matter that defies easy, definitive answers. Jesus' teaching is blunt, straightforward, and profoundly puzzling all at once. Our best hope is to place ourselves in the shoes of his original listeners and to imagine what they would have heard Jesus saying so we can understand their reactions.

The day after he multiplied bread, Jesus showed up in the synagogue of Capernaum where rumors surely buzzed about his latest miracle that called to mind Moses and the story of the exodus. Seizing the moment to test Jesus, the people challenged him to prove that he was as great as Moses. Rather than responding on their terms, Jesus challenged their misplaced priorities and understanding of God the Father. While the people credited Moses for providing their ancestors with bread, Jesus suggested that their error came by giving Moses too much credit. God the Father had provided that bread; Moses was merely an intermediary. If they had kept this straight, they wouldn't have compared Jesus with Moses or struggled to accept his teaching that he was "the bread of God . . . that comes down from heaven and gives life to the world" (John 6:33).

Much like the woman asking for water at the well in John 4, the people of Capernaum asking Jesus for bread clearly missed Jesus' point. Whether or not the people sincerely asked Jesus to give them this life-giving bread from heaven, we can assume that they were still thinking in literal terms. Having recently witnessed or at least heard strong evidence for his miracle with the loaves, they may have suspected that he had another miracle in store for them. Would Jesus give them the sign from heaven they'd been longing to see? No one would doubt him if he paired the miracle of the loaves with a definitive sign from heaven.

Once again, Jesus disappointed and confounded the crowd, claiming that *he* was the Bread of Life and that *he* had come down from heaven. While Jesus spoke of many other fascinating and important matters in John 6:35–40, the two great points of conflict had to do with his teaching about bread and his alleged origins from the Father. Jesus was trying to redirect the people's attention from physical bread and Moses to his Father and the Father's provision of life through him. It's likely that they wanted Jesus to literally rain manna down from heaven like Moses, something that rabbis from that time period fully expected to happen. This sign could have confirmed Jesus as their Messiah who would ensure they never had to worry about bread or the Romans ever again. The people were so consumed with their daily needs and future hopes for a Messiah that they could not accept Jesus' teaching that he wanted them to consume *him*. It would have been hard enough to convince the people to change their conceptions of Moses, but it's quite another thing for a would-be Messiah to tell the people to eat his body and to speak of God as "Father." Everything Jesus said put him far beyond what the people in Galilee were able to accept. Even for many today, we fully understand the original hearers' frustration when they replied, "This is a hard teaching. Who can accept it?" (John 6:60).

But Jesus wasn't just trying to confuse the Galileans. He was both downgrading Moses and elevating himself far above Moses to a position of striking intimacy with God. The people could not grasp Jesus' teaching about God the Father and his own origins in heaven. This bread was not what they were looking for, and they couldn't figure out what it meant to "eat" this bread or how this bread could keep them from hungering again.

The exchange mirrors again the conversation with the woman at the well, even though the conversation took a very different course. Much like the life-giving bread Jesus promised the Galileans, Jesus promised life-giving water that would always quench this woman's "thirst." In addition, after she received this message from Jesus and began to share it with others, Jesus refused food from his followers since he had "eaten" a different kind of food: doing his father's will (John 4:34). Just as the work of the Father sustained Jesus then, he also came to the people as the obedient Son of the Father (John 6:38), offering himself as life-sustaining bread.

Throughout the conversation with the people of Capernaum, an ongoing tension emerges concerning the role of Moses and the new teachings of Jesus. Those who put their trust in Moses were not necessarily seeking out the Father. In fact, Jesus had to invite them to come and believe, laying aside their preconceptions to share in the true bread that came down from heaven. This was asking a lot of the Jews who had centered their identity on being the chosen people led by Moses, freed on the Passover, and sustained by manna from heaven in the wilderness. When Jesus suggested that Moses hadn't actually seen God the Father or revealed him and that manna couldn't compare with himself, the bread of life that has come down from heaven, he dramatically challenged the Jews to rethink where they could find the life of God.

New Manna in the Wilderness

The most natural place to start with understanding this complex passage is in the exodus story and particularly in the Jewish Passover celebration that John noted at the start of this chapter as part of the story's backdrop. During the first celebration in Egypt, a Passover lamb was slaughtered in each household and the blood was smeared on the outside doorframes. As the lamb was eaten inside the home along with unleavened bread, the blood on the doorframe became a substitute for the plague of death that God sent to strike their Egyptian oppressors. The lamb that saved the Israelites from the plague was also the lamb they ate during the meal. As Jesus referenced his own saving work, he mixed these images with his own teaching about believing in him and abiding in him. Sitting at the table and eating the sacrificial Passover lamb and the unleavened bread provided rich imagery for accepting the living bread, which is Jesus, and "eating" or "believing in" him.

Jesus clearly saw his death in terms of the Passover observance since he shared the Passover meal with his disciples on the night before his death and spoke of the bread as his body broken for his disciples (Luke 22:19). Whether the image is water or bread, the general principle is the same: trust in Jesus and find life. Jesus freely offered this life to all who would come to him because his own story surpassed the exodus and Passover stories in every respect. He would offer the perfect sacrifice to save the people once and for all, and he would provide the perfect bread that would give them everlasting life.

As the people struggled to understand the teaching of Jesus about eating his body or how his body could be given for the life of the world, Jesus pushed the people's understanding of God beyond their limits; he also violated several other taboos. They weren't just invited to eat his body—the Bread of Life—they were also invited to drink his blood. In fact, if they refused his body and blood, they didn't have any life in themselves. As if to drive home his point, Jesus stated plainly, "For my flesh is real food and my blood is real drink" (John 6:55). By eating his body and drinking his blood, Jesus promised his listeners eternal life from the Father, something that Moses could not do through the manna.

When Jesus suggested that his blood should be drunk, he encouraged something that was explicitly condemned in the Old

Testament. The natural laws against drinking blood were clearly stipulated in the Jewish Law (Gen. 9:4; Lev. 3:17; 17:11; Deut. 12:23). The reason for the prohibition stemmed from the fact that a being's blood belonged to God alone. Because blood represents life and because God alone is the author and possessor of life, it is not permitted for other beings to partake of it. In fact, drinking blood was so reprehensible to Jewish sensibilities that it was prohibited among Gentiles when they began entering the church. This occurred even after Jesus and the Holy Spirit expressly rescinded the Jewish dietary laws (Mark 7; Acts 10), which seemingly included the prohibition of drinking blood. Old habits die hard, as the saying goes. Moreover, Jews associated drinking blood with witches and those who practiced sorcery. As Leviticus 19:26 says, "Do not eat any meat with the blood still in it. Do not practice divination or seek omens." The two are seen as going hand-in-hand.

Given this biblical and historical background, it is not difficult to recognize that this was the last straw for the people of Capernaum and for many of Jesus' would-be disciples. Even Jesus' closest disciples struggled enough with this teaching that Jesus questioned them, "You do not want to leave too, do you?" (John 6:67).

Peter provided the best and perhaps only resolution we'll ever find to this perplexing passage: "Lord, to whom shall we go? You have the words of eternal life. We have come to believe and to know that you are the Holy One of God" (John 6:68–69). Even as the crowds melted away and Jesus plummeted in popular opinion because of these scandalous teachings about his body and blood, Peter and the rest of the Twelve held on to what they knew about Jesus—albeit imperfectly. Even with Judas the traitor among them, they stood by their leader, putting their dreams of sitting on thrones by his side on hold for another day. They still weren't ready to let go of their aspirations. They also understood very little about the true identity of Jesus. In fact, they had been just as perplexed as the many who walked away. However, by enduring doubts and uncertainties, they remained close to Jesus, ensuring that they would one day taste the true Bread of Life.

WHAT KIND OF BREAD DO WE WANT?
Give Us Bread, Prosperity, Peace, Safety, and . . .

In Jesus' discourse in John 6, there is an ongoing tension between what Jesus offered and what his audience wanted. Whether it was his disciples' dreams of sitting on thrones or the dreams many had of a messiah who could provide for all of their needs, we routinely see Jesus offering the deeper life with God to people whose hands were too full of their own projects and plans. Perhaps they were too busy praying about the restoration of Israel that they missed God's offer to restore their lives.

I'm not expecting a messiah to come and deliver my nation from an occupying army or crushing tax that forces everyone to live in poverty, but I know something about asking God to take care of my problems. I sometimes approach prayer with an expectation that God just needs to take care of two or three problems and then I'll be able to relax and become more obedient. But the truth is that I'd just find something else to chase or worry about if God actually did provide for my requests each time I asked him. When I don't find satisfaction in the presence of Christ in my life or I ignore Jesus altogether, I'll inevitably find something to nibble on in the search for hope and contentment.

We've all watched a baby gnaw on a spoon. Gnawing on the spoon feels good if you have sore gums from teething, but the contentment that comes is more of a distraction than a solution to the core problem of hunger. I know all about distractions: gnawing on work, using new technology devices, or watching television in the search for contentment and peace. The list of prayer requests just gets longer and longer if I can't get the most important request right in the first place: to be satisfied in the Lord's presence.

The Importance of Sharing a Meal Together

Jesus frequently made important points about himself around tables and by using eating and drinking as key metaphors in his teaching. While we could say much about these images, there is something very personal and inviting about the approach Jesus took. Perplexing though his teachings may be, he was welcoming people to sit with him at his table. Whether a devout rabbi or a scheming tax collector, everyone has a place. Throughout his ministry, Jesus took steps to give more people a chance to sit at his table. The catch is that he didn't spare these people from his harder teachings. However, by inviting them to his table first, Jesus let them decide for themselves whether they felt drawn to him.

Whether we look at hospitality in our homes or being more open and welcoming in our churches, the challenge in this story is to be both welcoming and committed to sharing the message of Jesus in all of its complexity and difficulty.

Curiosity Isn't Enough

There was a fine line when it came to following Jesus. On the one hand, Jesus welcomed disciples who had doubts, questions, and imperfect theology about himself and about God the Father. On the other, he posed difficult questions and didn't back away from difficult teachings, such as this section about eating his body and drinking his blood. He may have even used this hard teaching to prompt the curious to make a tough decision: follow or leave.

There was little room for the half-interested and curious. Jesus far preferred someone with doubts and reservations yet who was willing to think hard and ask difficult questions over those who just wanted to enjoy the perks of being associated with a messiah. He wasn't deluded into thinking that large crowds marked the success of his movement. In fact, he did everything he could to challenge the crowds to take his teachings seriously, regardless of the consequences. He showed no hesitation to lose potential followers for the sake of focusing on those few who were committed to thinking through his message and learning how to live it out.

This is not typically the way we approach ministry today. Leaders feel pressure to keep numbers high and to please as many people as possible. Losing attendees and members and not making things easy for any guests who might visit one's community is equated with failure and lack of health. There are plenty of leaders who feel pressure to keep growing the numbers of people in their ministries because they've been told a "healthy" ministry grows much like a healthy plant grows, starting out like a small seed but growing into a large bush or tree. In addition, church members wonder what's wrong with their ministries when people leave and their numbers dwindle. While losing members could certainly be a sign of problems and unhealthy rhythms at a church, it is also the case that the demands of the gospel and the difficult teachings of Jesus are sometimes too disruptive and uncompromising for people to effortlessly assimilate into their lives. Perhaps there are churches that have a problem with "too much growth" today. If the message of Jesus is too appealing, perhaps it's appropriate to ask if we're backing away from the more troublesome passages like John 6 where Jesus unapologetically told his followers to eat his body and drink his blood — regardless of how many people may or may not continue attending one's ministry.

At the same time, church leaders also feel great pressure to avoid discussions about doubt or Bible passages that don't have easy answers. While leaders aren't necessarily tasked with disrupting the faith of their churches, there is something to be said for creating an atmosphere where church members can wrestle with tough questions and follow Jesus without necessarily having all of the answers. Jesus took a long-view approach to his disciples, working with their doubts and their unfinished theology. Even if Peter believed that Jesus was indeed the Messiah, Peter was still very far from fully understanding what it meant to be the Messiah. Peter didn't exactly tell Jesus that he had it all figured out when he responded to Jesus' question about them turning away. He simply said, "Where else will we go?" The discipleship process has room for imperfect theology and enough patience to handle doubts. The one essential is a desire to draw near to Jesus and to obey him, even when mysteries and uncertainties remain.

We say all of this without insinuating that certainty or security in one's faith are bad things. Jesus promises to send the Spirit to help us understand him better, and therefore he expects us to move toward a clearer understanding over time. If anything,

Jesus challenges those who are uncommitted and certain while welcoming the committed and uncertain.

JESUS IS STILL THE BREAD OF LIFE

Christians have made a connection between Jesus' discourse in John 6 and the partaking of the Lord's Supper since the days of the early church in the Roman Empire. During the Lord's Supper, a Christian symbolically consumes Jesus' "flesh" by eating broken bread and takes in his "blood" by drinking juice or wine. Although this practice is ordinary for Christians, especially those who have attended church since childhood, this meal is strange for non-Christians and those with little or no previous church background. In fact, since Roman times, some non-Christians familiar with this practice considered it not just strange, but revolting. For all they knew, the Christians were literally consuming the flesh and blood of some man who had died as a criminal. From their perspective, in other words, the early Christians practiced cannibalism. Rather than finding this practice compelling and life-giving, they rejected the new Christian religion as sickening and opposed to natural law and common decency.

Such a mind-set, however foreign this may sound for Christians today, is actually closer to how Jesus' original hearers would have understood Jesus' discourse. For Jews during the first century, the consumption of flesh and the drinking of blood opposed the laws of nature, let alone were prohibited by the Old Testament. Jesus' words were a stumbling block to the people's understanding of right and wrong, and it is therefore not surprising that many of his followers walked away from their rabbi at this "hard teaching." In fact, what is perhaps most surprising in this passage is that the people did not try to stone Jesus for advancing what sounded to them like sacrilegious teaching.

Within the Christian fold, the "hard teaching" of Jesus in the Lord's Supper is the diversity of opinion regarding how it is to be practiced and interpreted. Since the Protestant Reformation, in particular, Christians have not only vigorously disagreed with each other on how to practice this commanded meal, but they have even killed and died over it. It is, of course, a great tragedy that a meal meant to give life has been the cause of so much taking and losing of it.

We will never know the precise way to practice the Lord's Supper and there will never be conformity within the church. Some people may abandon one church for another or even reject the Christian faith altogether because of the lack of consensus and because it is a practice that is countercultural in so many ways. For whatever takes place in this symbolic meal, it is a mystery that defies rational explanation. As a church, when we practice this ritual, we lay aside our education, ethnicity, and socioeconomic status, and we join with our brothers and sisters in the life and the hope to come through Jesus Christ. Without fully understanding what is going on, we consume the bread that represents the One who really does give life and who really does love the church enough to be broken and die for it.

■5 THE RICH YOUNG RULER

A MESSIAH WHO MAKES LIFE EASY

Antony grew up in a wealthy Christian home with his sister. Tragedy struck when their parents passed away during Antony's teen years, and he then became responsible for the substantial inheritance they left behind, not to mention caring for his sister. Over the following years, Antony heard a sermon about the rich young ruler being challenged to sell everything and follow Jesus. Something stirred in his heart, and he knew what he needed to do.

After ensuring that his sister had her needs provided for, Antony sold everything he owned, gave the money to the poor, and moved out into the desert in Egypt. He spent his days working, fasting, and praying in extreme solitude. Soon word of this unusual man spread throughout the city, and visitors sought out Antony, seeking his advice and prayers. Over time he had to move farther into the wilderness just to avoid the crowds that came seeking his wisdom. Many reported that Antony saw visions of angels, performed miracles, and even predicted the arrival of certain visitors.

The stories about Antony also include some extremely unusual encounters with demons that left him beaten and wounded. Other times visitors would come and find him arguing with demons, ordering them to leave. Despite these harrowing encounters, Antony sparked a movement of Christians into the desert, leading to the formation of many monastic communities. Antony and his fellow monks found peace and joy in the solitude of the desert, leaving behind collections of wisdom that have endured for centuries until this very day. We know Antony today as Saint Antony, a desert father from the fourth century in Egypt.[1] It's difficult to imagine leaving everything behind quite as dramatically as he did, and yet his story isn't necessarily an anomaly. You don't have to be a monk in the desert to figure out the benefits of selling your possessions.

Even outside the Christian monastic world today, there is a movement toward simplicity and downsizing. In an opinion piece for *The New York Times*, entrepreneur Graham Hill wrote about his move from several large homes to a single, 420-square-foot apartment. In his days of affluence, he bought large homes he didn't need and filled them with stuff that left him dissatisfied. Over time the weight of these many possessions became a source of stress. Selling most of his possessions wasn't really even a sacrifice; he found it immensely liberating.[2]

The same ironic struggle with money is common among lottery winners. *This American Life* reported a story about Ed Ugel who used to "buy" the prizes from lottery winners by exchanging a lower lump sum of cash for the more spread-out lottery payments that could take twenty years to materialize. Ugel noted that lottery winners often believed the hype that they were millionaires and started to make poor choices that landed them in hot water financially even though the yearly payout could easily replace a typical middle-income job. Overwhelming car payments, ill-fated investments in restaurant startups, and huge mortgages all hurt these new "millionaires" and left them in worse financial shape than before they struck it rich. Ugel spoke of winning the lottery as a kind of cancer that rarely helped anyone. There was something about the perception of having great wealth that prompted these winners to make losing choices. Ugel found that many of them were willing to sell their prizes for less money just to move on with their lives.[3]

Whether we're speaking of a fourth-century mystic fasting in the desert and fighting demons or about today's millionaires who can't get rid of their money fast enough, we can see that money can often create more problems than it solves. Once your basic financial needs are provided for, money can prove counterproductive. In fact, research based on American standards of living has shown that income levels above $75,000 to $100,000 rarely make a significant impact on overall well-being or happiness.[4]

As we look at the story of the rich young ruler and weigh Jesus' demand to sell everything and give it to the poor, we typically end up struggling with one of two responses: Either we think Jesus was completely unreasonable with this man, or we begin to worry about our own attachments to possessions. As we place ourselves in the story, we end up feeling either frustrated with Jesus or ashamed of our own materialism. Perhaps we have a mix of both. The anecdotes above about monks, entrepreneurs, and lottery winners suggest another way to enter this story: What if this is a story about liberation and freedom?

While we can't perfectly recreate the scene or truly know what this young ruler really thought, let's set up a few ground rules. First, let's begin by recreating the scene, the theology, and the social norms within which this story takes place. Second, we need to shelve our own anxieties for a moment to look at Jesus' message for this particular man. Once we can catch a sharper glimpse of this exchange, we'll be in far better shape.

NOT ALMS, EVERYTHING[5]

A Theology of Wealth

From the perspective of the rich young ruler, God had been quite good to him. Everyone thought that at the time. Throughout the Gospels, we see a thread in Jewish thought that prosperity equaled blessing, and any affliction that brought on poverty had to be a punishment from God because of sin in a person's life or family. The blind man Jesus healed was written off as an unreliable witness because everyone automatically categorized him as a wicked sinner "steeped in sin" since his birth.

By the same token, any kind of misfortune in life could be blamed on the presence of sin. When Jesus explained the justice of God to his disciples, he called to mind a recent catastrophe where a tower fell on a crowd of people. While conventional wisdom wrote off these unfortunate victims as sinners worthy of judgment, Jesus leveled the playing field by pointing out that they were not necessarily worse sinners than anyone else in the land. Jesus rejected their theology of wealth and blessing without necessarily offering an alternative. If anything, he clouded matters rather than providing clarity. It wasn't for them to know the ways of God or the reasons behind tragedies or blessings.

The rich young ruler didn't need to tell Jesus that he'd faithfully obeyed the commandments. His credentials spoke to God's approval. Why would God give a sinner so much prosperity? Such thinking woefully simplified the theology of the Old Testament, especially the Psalms and Prophets. While every blessing and good thing ultimately comes from a good Creator, the prosperity of the wicked is presented as a disturbing mystery. Rather than offering a system for blessings and curses, the Psalms and Prophets reveal the same kind of complexity that Jesus brought to the rich young ruler, the crowds, and his disciples (see Ps. 73:3–5; 94:3; Jer. 12:1–2). Jesus spoke against any overly simplistic theological system for interpreting the Bible where the righteous are always blessed. As the rich young ruler bowed before Jesus, full of assumptions and confidence, no one was prepared for what happened next.

What the Rich Young Ruler Wanted

Why did people go to meet Jesus? Throughout the Gospels, people generally approached Jesus for one of three reasons: to ask him for help, to follow him, or to confront him. The rich young ruler doesn't really fit into any of these categories. He wasn't sick or demon-possessed. He seemed an unlikely candidate for a disciple, since he had no intention of letting go of his wealth and power. And rather than confront Jesus, he approached him with reverence, respectfully addressing him as a rabbi. He wasn't looking for a fight. He didn't have a theological position to test out. He didn't have any intentions of rocking the boat in his own life or for Jesus.

What did he want? In a word, he wanted validation.

This ruler wouldn't have approached Jesus unless he had all of his bases covered—at least the outward rules that anyone could measure easily. He wasn't a murderer, thief, adulterer, fraud, or disobedient son. No one would stand up and speak against him. He had an air-tight case before Jesus. All he needed was Jesus' validation to achieve the latest notch in his belt that would further cement his standing among God and people. In addition, he wanted to know that he was on the right path in his religious observance. While he wasn't all that interested in changing his practices, he was more than happy for Jesus to approve of him. With the thumbs-up from Jesus, he could return to his comfortable home knowing that he truly had it all: comfort, power, and the approval of God's prophet. He soon found out that the latter wasn't attained quite as easily as he'd thought.

What Jesus Wanted

It's possible to see Jesus in a negative light in this story. Shouldn't he have reached out to this young man to help him? Maybe he needed the slow track to discipleship. Why wasn't Jesus more patient?

Taking the young man's motivations into account, we can see that he wasn't necessarily interested even in the slow track to discipleship. If anything, he wanted a label he could affix to himself: "Approved by Jesus." He didn't want the lifestyle that Jesus offered. He wasn't ready to treat Jesus as his Lord, since he was the ruler. He had no intention of letting Jesus compete as the ruler of his life or anything else that concerned him.

With this in mind, we can understand Jesus' position. He couldn't give this man the pat on the back he wanted. That would be deceptive and ultimately harmful for his other disciples by validating their distorted theology about wealth while also under-cutting his own message about whole-life commitment to loving God and others. In fact, Jesus may have done the best thing he could to make this man a disciple: challenge him with an impossible offer that showed how seriously he took discipleship.

At the time of Jesus, there was a long-standing tradition of students seeking out a rabbi and becoming a disciple. Jesus broke with convention at times by calling his disciples and by including women among his disciples—something he affirmed quite dramatically by letting Mary, the sister of Martha, learn from him during a meal at their home. While Jesus didn't choose his disciples the conventional way, he wasn't above using culturally recognized ways of testing the commitment of would-be disciples by shunning a prospective disciple. By making such a steep demand of this young ruler, Jesus could have been testing him to see if he would go home and reconsider his decision. We can't imagine Jesus turning away this young man if they crossed paths in the future and the man earnestly desired to become a disciple. While we can't know for certain what Jesus intended, his startling demand had a precedent in the culture.

Jesus' challenge to the rich young ruler is directly tied to his questions, "Teacher, what good thing must I do to get eternal life?" and "What do I still lack?" The conversation proves challenging to us today on several levels, especially for Protestants who are always on the lookout for "works of righteousness" that "earn" salvation. Why would Jesus tell this man he only needed to obey the commandments and to sell his possessions? Here again is the tension of grace and sanctification. God's favor can never be earned, but we have a choice each day to draw near to

God or to follow our own courses. The concept of eternal life in the gospel of John isn't only a future event. It's an ongoing experience of God's life now and forever. So Jesus tells this man that the only way to experience the life of God is to live a holy life. The way Jesus presented this answer with, "You know the commandments," suggests that every Jew knew that obedience leads to life, while disobedience cuts us off from the life that God freely gives. However, when the young man pressed his point, opening his life up to the scrutiny of Jesus, he wasn't prepared for how personal Jesus' request would be.

Far from viewing Jesus as a harsh religious leader making angry demands of his would-be followers, Jesus offered to take care of this man and to give him life. "Come follow me" seems like a risky move after selling everything, but what if Jesus was offering this young man the safest possible place?[6] If the man really wanted eternal life and even perfection, then Jesus offered him the best alternative. It's not that owning possessions will automatically keep anyone from heaven. Rather, they are great hindrances, symptoms of our greed, and weights that can hold us back.

If we can read Jesus' answers without necessarily reading too much into them, Jesus cut right to the heart of the issue. This young man knew the commandments and what the law said about loving God and loving others. He didn't need Jesus to spell it out for him. However, he wasn't satisfied with Jesus' response. He wanted validation from Jesus and a unique status that set him apart from others, and so he pressed Jesus further with his question about what he lacked.

Jesus actually offered him the surest path to freedom and eternal life. If he wanted to overcome the greed that could keep him away from eternal life, he had to lighten up—literally. Jesus wasn't trying to disqualify him. Jesus gave him a chance to be free from the possessions that held him hostage. While the rich young man thought he had his act together before God, Jesus suggested that the very possessions that supposedly made him blessed were most likely liabilities that could hold him back from God and the eternal life he craved. The rich young man could not find perfection or eternal life easily with so many possessions.

Did Jesus want to send this man away? Perhaps he did, but only if the man refused his invitation to follow him. We see this "invitation" and count it as anything but that today. However, Jesus diagnosed this man's problem, and we do ourselves a disservice if we minimize its severity. He not only had a divided heart between God and his wealthy position, he also couldn't understand what God asks of his people. From his perspective, he never did anything all that bad. In fact, he'd obeyed all of the commandments. Jesus shattered that illusion by showing him the grip of greed and money on his life.

Packing Our Camels

Jesus wasn't offering a conventional approach to spirituality. In fact, Jewish teachers did not really endorse selling all of your possessions, since children were expected to care for their parents. Giving away all of your money ensured that you'd never be able to meet your cultural or family obligations. Much like the man who said he would follow Jesus after burying his parents, the rich young ruler landed right in the middle of a perfect storm, between the values of his time and Jesus' demands for commitment.

Christians have debated whether this passage teaches that every disciple of Jesus should leave his or her possessions behind and give them to the poor. However, there are two elements to the New Testament that will help us sort out this story. First, there was no way for this rich young ruler to actually follow Jesus without leaving everything behind. And even if he did start following Jesus full time without selling all of his possessions, he would have been worried and distracted. Much like Peter, John, and Matthew who all left their careers behind, this young man would need to focus his entire energy on the literal task of following Jesus from town to town if he wanted to be perfect and overcome every barrier that could keep him from God.

Second, leaving everything was not necessarily mandatory for every disciple. Some wealthy women traveled with Jesus and supported him out of their own pockets. From this we conclude that wealth alone did not preclude anyone from following Jesus. Each person was different. For a select few, money was not a distraction from being a disciple; in fact, it was even an asset. We read in the book of Acts, for example, of Christians of great wealth serving as patrons for the early church. For many others, however, including this rich young man, wealth was more than a distraction. It was an idol that had to be completely jettisoned to follow Jesus.

HELLO SIMPLICITY

The story of the rich young ruler is one of the most disruptive and disturbing stories in the New Testament, especially for North American Christians who are disproportionally wealthy in relation to the rest of the world. We all fear the possibility that our possessions and lifestyles will keep us from loving God and serving others. As we seek ways to let this story shape us today, we should remain wary of two extremes: one that makes it sinful to own anything and the other that writes off this story as a one-time event that can't possibly apply to us today. This story challenges us to consider the cost of following Jesus and what we should be willing to give up to follow him. In a word, that would be everything. Everything is on the table for a disciple, but that doesn't mean a disciple can't own a table.

As we look at some possible implications for this story, we must pay attention to the points that cause uneasiness or ring particularly true.

Who Is Blessed by God?

When I started a new job a few years back, I had a rough first year. Nothing worked out and my income dipped. We weren't going to make it financially, and I had a lot of conversations with God about my plummeting bank account. Why wasn't God blessing my work? Could I be doing something wrong that caused God to withhold material blessings from me?

When I asked a friend for some help, she pointed out a rather obvious failure on my part. My entire strategy was wrong. It took time to right things in my work, but I'd over-spiritualized a professional mistake, confusing it with God's blessings or curses.

Do we tend to measure blessings with material and social markers? Do we admire the wealthy as blessed and the poor as cursed or lazy? The bias of affluence is hard to shake. Who hasn't wondered about God's approval or mercy when going through a hard time? It's easy to think that God isn't present when life is hard. The Psalms are full of such pleas for God's blessing in the midst of trouble.

This story about Jesus and the rich young ruler smashes any templates we may want to create around the spirituality of material blessings. For starters, money and possessions can just as easily become liabilities that keep us from God and from doing his will. For instance, the extreme example of the entrepreneur at the start of this chapter illustrates how owning more requires more maintenance. If you own a swimming pool, you need to spend time testing and treating the water. If you own a large property, you have to mow the lawn and landscape it. If you have technology, you'll have to spend time and money fixing it. If you buy a large house with extra rooms, you'll need to furnish and clean them. Everything we add to our lives demands time from us, time that takes us away from more pressing matters like loving and serving others.

More stuff does not equal a greater blessing. While God can and does bless us with material possessions at times, the measure for a life well lived is in learning to abide in Christ and to devote our lives to gaining treasure in heaven. Whether in plenty or want, our goal remains the same: to remain in Christ alone.

Why Do We Follow Jesus?

We all think we know the correct answer to the question of why we should follow Jesus. However, Christianity takes shape in the way we live each day, not in the answers we know. I have caught myself frequently treating God more as a genie bound to grant my wishes than as the Lord of my life.

The great challenge of following Jesus is that we have to trust that giving up everything we want is the best thing for us. There is a particularly frightening moment when we let go of our desires and offer our possessions to God with open hands and we have no guarantees about what awaits us. In a sense, we have to empty our hands of what we hold on to in order to receive what God will give us. However, as we let go of our own plans and possessions, we'll experience the tension of living only with Christ since we don't know what the future holds or what our next steps will be. Once our hands are empty and open, we'll have every reason to listen to Jesus for direction and receive what he gives us. I've found that what I receive from Christ proves far better than any other plan I could dream up on my own. I just have to pass through a time of uncertainty to arrive there.[7]

These moments will come repeatedly in our lives. We'll let go of our plans, depend on Christ alone, and then receive direction, but it won't be long before we'll have to let go of our plans once again. The irony is that we struggle to follow Jesus because we fear he won't give us what we want; yet oftentimes what we want is not best for us. Rather than rejecting God because he does not give us what we want, we have to recognize that much of what he gives us is better than what we desire. And when he does not give us what we want, he always stands with us in our pain and waiting.

Disciples of Jesus learn that the true prize is Christ alone, and that having him changes how we perceive what we have and don't have. The rich young ruler could only see what Jesus would take away from him, but a disciple sees that having Jesus is greater than any position, treasure, or property. We follow Jesus because he loved us first, because he is our vine connecting us to the Father, and because he calls us his brothers and sisters in the family of God.

What Must I Do to Inherit Eternal Life?

Perhaps our discomfort with this story comes from our own backgrounds. Many Christians today, in America at least, have asked this same question at one time or another. We want to know how to inherit eternal life. Who doesn't? Many of us probably grew up hearing sermons where preachers posed this very question. After hearing these sermons, there's a good chance that many of us bowed our heads to pray some kind of salvation prayer, perhaps on multiple occasions, just to be sure that we had eternal life locked in. We all want to know how to be 100 percent certain that we have eternal life.

Jesus offers us the closest thing to an answer: leave your possessions and follow me. In other words, you can be reasonably certain that you have eternal life if you make decisions that demonstrate a complete commitment to God's priorities and rewards. The greater hold possessions have on your life, the more conflict you'll have with Jesus as the Lord of your life. The more you invest in loving God and neighbors, acting as if these are the things that will actually bring rewards from God, the more likely you've had a Spirit-led encounter with the living God.

A NEW TAKE ON POSSESSIONS

If there's one thing this story can teach us, it's that our possessions and personal goals can become obstacles that keep us from God, even if they're not "evil" or wrong in and of themselves. Oftentimes the urgent and less-important things of life can crowd out still, quiet moments with God and any time that we could spend serving others. If something is a priority, we make time for it.

We don't have to purge our garages and basements immediately to faithfully follow Jesus. Why not start with a simple question, "What is keeping me from following Jesus?" Is something keeping you from serving the poor in your neighborhood? Are there constraints on your time or space that keep you from prayer?

A friend of mine recently rearranged his bedroom to add a sitting chair and then started waking up earlier to make more time for prayer. A pastor I know started inviting a lonely man from the neighborhood to the church office to help and hang out with anyone who stops by—they get less work done, but this man feels like he has a family for the first time in his life. For me personally, I've found that praying on the hour each day helps force me to make prayer a higher priority and gives me Scripture to chew on during the day. By the same token, I struggle to find the balance between my need for leisure and family compared to the time I can give to serving my neighbors. I can see how easily my life and home can become cluttered with stuff. Each new piece of technology I pick up chips away at my time. Commercials and ads remind me of all the things I don't own. Even the products that promise simplicity are still another thing to buy and use.

As long as we hold on to our dreams and possessions tightly, we'll always search for validation. There will always be an uneasy feeling that something isn't quite right. We may even seek out Jesus and ask for his blessing on our lives as they are rather than asking him how they should be. The most validating truth we can know is that Jesus loves and welcomes us, and we alone can only disqualify ourselves—whether that's through the things we own or the ways we perceive ourselves.

This isn't a story about how much we're allowed to own. This is a story about whether we have a hold on Jesus or our possessions have a hold on us. We have a contrast between pleasures that are temporal and passing away and the abundant life we can experience now and forever.

Jesus isn't condemning us because we own computers, cars, and homes. He isn't out to make discipleship impossible. He's throwing us a lifeline that can pull us into the kingdom if we're willing to let go of whatever we're holding and cling only to him.

NOTES

1. Henry L. Carrigan, ed., *The Wisdom of the Desert Fathers and Mothers*, Paraclete Essentials (Brewster, Mass.: Paraclete, 2010), 1–76.

2. Graham Hill, "Living with Less. A Lot Less," *The New York Times*, March 9, 2013, http://www.nytimes.com/2013/03/10/opinion/sunday/living-with-less-a-lot-less.html?pagewanted=1&_r=0&ref=general&src=me.

3. Ira Glass, "Nice Work if You Can Get It," *This American Life*, April 6, 2007, http://www.thisamericanlife.org/radio-archives/episode/329/transcript.

4. Bradley Wright, *Upside: Surprising Good News about the State of Our World* (Grand Rapids, Mich.: Bethany, 2011), 123–124. See also the original 2010 study out of Princeton University: Daniel Kahneman and Angus Deaton, "High Income Improves Evaluation of Life but Not Emotional Well-Being," *Proceedings of the National Academy of Sciences of the United States of America* 107, no. 38 (2010), http://www.pnas.org/content/107/38/16489.

5. This section title comes from W. D. Davies and D. C. Allison, *Matthew 8–18*, Vol. 2, International Critical Commentary (New York: Bloomsbury, 1997), 46.

6. My pastor Jeff Cannell at Central Vineyard Church in Columbus, Ohio, suggested that we read this story as Jesus compassionately offering this young man a way to live "footloose and fancy-free."

7. For more about this process, see our book *Hazardous: Committing to the Cost of Following Jesus* (Fort Washington, Pa.: CLC, 2012).

■6 JUDAS ISCARIOT

A MESSIAH WHO FOLLOWS MY PLANS

Josephus wasn't a popular man among the Romans. Neither was he respected among his first-century Jewish countrymen. To the Romans, who generally ignored his works of Jewish history, he was a Jewish rebel who luckily won the favor of a Roman general. To the Jews, he was an elite aristocrat, disconnected from the common people, who sold out his people during the Jewish War in 66–70 A.D. In other words, no one liked Josephus because he was a traitor.

Looking back on Josephus, we can see that he was indeed an opportunist consumed with his own self-preservation, but we can also sympathize with him to a certain degree. Not too many of us have been caught up in a national rebellion against a superior army! Raised in an aristocratic home and swept up into the Jewish rebellion against Rome, it's likely that he wasn't the most enthusiastic freedom fighter among his contemporaries. In fact, it's possible that he received little to no military training when compared to his Roman counterparts. He was most likely a Pharisee and trusted member of the ruling elite who were trying to bring the radicals in Galilee under some semblance of centralized command during a hopeless rebellion. Instead, Josephus and his troops lost key battles and wound up surrounded in a cave. We don't know how he managed to emerge from the cave without committing suicide like the rest of his men, but that wasn't his only lucky break. Josephus prophesied that Vespasian, the Roman general who had bested him, would one day rise to become Caesar. So Vespasian decided to spare Josephus's life. If the story of *Macbeth* offers any hints about the human condition, it's that ambitious men don't need too much encouragement to start a rebellion. Remarkably, within a few years of Josephus's prophecy, Vespasian became Caesar. With his prophetic value confirmed, Josephus enjoyed freedom under the patronage of Vespasian.

Josephus was smart enough to know that he couldn't rely on prophecies for the rest of his career. He wasn't willing to die for his country. His training as a Pharisee wouldn't do him any good in the Roman camp. Therefore, in the interest of self-preservation, Josephus acted as a translator and negotiator for the Roman forces as they laid siege to Jerusalem and Masada. It's quite likely that his wife and many of his relatives were killed during the siege of Jerusalem, and therefore his defection to Rome represented a definitive cutting of ties with the Jewish people. When the war in Israel was over, he moved to Rome, where he reinvented himself once again, this time as a historian who explained the Jewish people for a Roman audience.

After completing a bloody conquest in Israel that used up a tremendous number of resources, the majority of the Roman people were uninterested in what Josephus, Vespasian's Jewish prophet, had to say. By the same token, the Jewish people left behind to pick up the pieces in the devastated land of Israel didn't take kindly to Josephus's version of the Jewish War, where a group of seditious brigands brought down the wrath of God on the land in the form of an invading army. In other words, Josephus argued that the Romans became God's chosen instruments of judgment, much like the Babylonians and Assyrians of the past—only he claimed the Romans were more virtuous and kindhearted. For Josephus, this line of thinking both preserved his reputation as a member of the "victimized" Jewish aristocracy and justified the brutal actions of his patrons.

While we can't blame Josephus for trying to preserve his life in an impossible situation, he has been regarded with a measure of suspicion by scholars who question his reliability as a historical source. If he only wanted to save his own neck, he had something a bit stronger than a bias clouding his presentation of events. He wasn't an academic scholar writing for tenure. He was writing to save his life.

Loyalty to a government or nation is one thing, but there is far more at stake when it comes to our loyalty to God. While we can look back at the ruins of Rome and recognize the passing nature of earthly kingdoms, our allegiance to the Creator of the world is a far more serious matter. Opposing God isn't a matter of objecting to a government on the basis of conscience or political divisions. When we place greater value in preserving our own goals than following the will of our Creator, we perpetuate a cycle of brokenness that has defined human history. Choosing our own way over God's won't give us the freedom, peace, and control that we think it will.

CHOOSING SIDES

The Judas Prayer

Many of the prayers I've heard Christians pray over the years, myself included, decide beforehand what God desires for our lives. I've even added a holiness topping: "If you give me more money, I'll donate more to an orphanage." It's like twisting God's arm so he'll go along with "the plan."

If there was anyone in the gospel narratives who clung to his own plan, it was Judas Iscariot (we'll call him Judas from here on out). We don't generally spend a lot of time talking about Judas, because he committed an unfathomable act of treachery. However, if we step back for a second look, we may find a character who makes us squirm a little because he's just a bit too familiar. Before Judas betrayed Jesus, he was looking for a messiah who would let him follow his own plans.

When Judas Iscariot, the disciple of Jesus, mouthed the Lord's Prayer, especially when it came time to say, "Your will be done," perhaps he voiced this prayer with the assumption that God's will paralleled his own. We have probably all been guilty of that sin before.

But what happens when God's will differs from our own? What happens when the fulfillment of the prayer, that is, the part when God's will is accomplished, flies in the face of our will?

A Messiah Who Did Not Follow Judas's Plan

Judas may be the most intriguing of Jesus' disciples. He is certainly the most elusive. Over the centuries, Christians have characterized him, some maliciously so, in any number of ways: He was a heartless miser, a power-hungry schemer, a green-eyed apprentice overshadowed by a more-talented master.

Maybe, but maybe not. Perhaps we should more modestly characterize Judas as a man who initially latched onto the magnetic personality of Jesus but eventually became disillusioned as Jesus' vision for the messiahship began to contrast considerably with Judas's vision. Judas, like all of the disciples and many others in the first century, had prematurely filled in the bullet points of the Messiah's job description. And when Jesus the Messiah failed to fulfill the obligations Judas had imposed on him, he craftily bailed out when there was still time.

There is good reason to believe that Judas was the most perceptive—"shrewd as a snake," we might say—of Jesus' disciples. He may have been the first one to recognize the implications of Jesus' upside-down kingdom. Although it was Peter who first confessed Jesus as the Messiah, he incorrectly assumed that messiahship equaled military rule. But perhaps Judas was the first of Jesus' disciples to realize that Jesus' intentions for the messiahship embraced nothing pertaining to physical rebellion. Jesus' kingdom was not of this world, after all.

Realizing this before the other disciples did, and presupposing that all of them had risked their livelihoods and reputations for Jesus, Judas decided to incriminate his rabbi before it was too late. During their last week together in Jerusalem in celebration of the Jewish festival of Passover, on which occasion Jesus brought his ministry to crescendo, Jesus aggressively unpacked his teachings and did not mince words as he had done outside the Holy City. As Jesus did so, he openly defied—in fact, condemned—the religious establishment to such an extent that he made his death inevitable.

It's possible, though not advisable, to criticize the temple and flout the Sabbath laws in faraway Galilee, but it's different to openly disrupt the temple system and criticize it in person, as well as heal people on the Sabbath in front of the religious leaders whose responsibility it was to judge those who violated the Jewish Law. Jesus made enemies when he was in Jerusalem, and Judas, as astute as he was, knew it. It's possible that some of Jesus' other disciples also flirted with betraying their master after their stint in Jerusalem. Within a few hours of Judas's betrayal, in fact, practically all of Jesus' disciples—even Peter—scattered like sheep without a shepherd.

It was the most infamous disbanding of a group in world history. When one's life is on the line, loyalty wavers. Unlike Judas, who knew exactly what was going on, the response of the other disciples evidenced their surprise at the betrayal, and their actions were clearly not premeditated. Peter wanted to fight; Mark ran away without his clothes; John watched from a distance; and the others may have quietly left the scene.

When Our Will Collides with God's

We essentially have two options when God does not follow our plan for life: going our own way or readjusting our course. On the night when Jesus was arrested, Judas had already made his decision to go his own way. That is to say, at some point in his apprenticeship to Jesus, he rejected his master and decided to cash out his chips while he still had a hand to play.

This gambling metaphor, unfortunately, applies all too well to Jesus' last days. Judas was not the only one with a hand in this high-stakes situation. All of the major players in the condemnation of Jesus were shrewd gamblers. First, there was the Jewish high priest, a man named Caiaphas. He famously declared that it was better for one man to die on behalf of all others. He gambled on the assumption that Jesus' death would quell the possibility of rebellion among the people during the frenzied season of Passover, when Jews reenacted how God saved them from their pagan overlords centuries before and who were on the prowl for someone, such as this messianic figure from Nazareth, to foment an uprising.

Then there was a Roman prefect named Pontius Pilate. He must have surely resented being compelled to leave his balmy and breezy home on the Mediterranean coast for a Jewish festival just as much as he loathed being the Roman governor of a minor and obstinate province in the first place. Reluctantly, he gambled on the assumption that the death of Jesus would keep the peace in Jerusalem and, by extension, would keep him in the good graces of the Roman emperor. Additionally, even the Roman soldiers got in on the action, as they famously cast lots for Jesus' clothes.

Finally, of course, there was Judas. Unlike Jesus' other disciples, Judas was an experienced player. The fact that Jesus designated him, of all the other capable disciples — Matthew the tax collector included — as the treasurer of the group's finances suggests that Judas was shrewd and astute. Jesus had actually focused much of his teaching on parables about money. And although he clearly denounced the love of money as a serious sin, he also praised those who were good with it. This is clear, for example, in his parables of the shrewd manager, the just steward, and the talents. As Jesus' steward of money, Judas must have been a sharp manager. But according to the gospel of John, Judas's serpentine shrewdness was not joined with the innocence of a dove.

The majority of the four gospels in the New Testament place Judas's betrayal of Jesus immediately after a woman wandered into a room full of men laying on couches as they ate, which was the tradition for parties, and rubbed expensive perfume on Jesus. This was a scandalous act. Naturally, the disciples did not approve of the woman's actions. Without even commenting on her shocking, though surely sincere, decision to rub the expensive perfume on Jesus' feet with her own hair, the disciples must have been acutely sensitive to the extreme poverty they had experienced in Jerusalem the past few days. Rather than seeing heartfelt devotion, they saw unbridled excess. Judas, perhaps because he was the treasurer, voiced publicly what the others were saying amongst themselves. "Why this waste? . . . This perfume could have been sold at a high price and the money given to the poor" (Matt. 26:8–9).

Judas was probably thinking of Jesus' words just a day before at the temple. As Jesus and his disciples sat opposite the treasury and watched person after person put money into the charity box, Jesus drew attention to a "poor widow" who had only thrown in two small coins, roughly "worth only a few cents" (Mark 12:42). Rather than pointing a finger at her to denounce her actions as shameful, which Jesus had already done that week to others, Jesus praised the sacrificial nature of her donation. However, Judas apparently paid more attention to her extreme poverty than her sacrificial act. As Jesus himself said, "This poor widow has put more into the treasury than all the others" (Mark 12:43).

Knowing this, Judas must have been outraged when the opposite occurred the following day. Instead of a poor widow giving away all she had to live on, in walked an uninvited wealthy woman who extravagantly, just as much as she did provocatively, poured the equivalent of almost a year's salary on Jesus' body. And instead of condemning her, Jesus actually commended her. In fact, Jesus described her act in a way that surely must have silenced the room: "When she poured this perfume on my body, she did it to prepare me for burial" (Matt. 26:12). To make matters even more controversial, Jesus went on to say, perhaps intended directly for Judas, "Truly I tell you, wherever this gospel is preached throughout the world, what [this woman] has done will also be told, in memory of her" (Matt. 26:13).

Judas had seen enough. Whatever game plan Jesus was following as the Messiah, it differed from Judas's.

It's hard to not overemphasize how different Judas was from Jesus and his disciples. If Judas Iscariot's last name indicates where he originated, as it probably does, he may have been Jesus' only disciple who came from Judea rather than Galilee. If so, we could surmise that Judas may have been more distant from Jesus than the others. Judas probably had a different regional accent—unlike Peter's, for instance, which immediately implicated him as a Galilean and therefore a companion of Jesus—and the other disciples may have held different views on the role of the Messiah from a Judean like Judas. Whatever the case, Judas gradually recognized Jesus' strategy for revealing the kingdom of God, and he did not like it.

It's very likely that this incident of the perfume anointing was simply the culmination of many contributing factors. A general list of Jesus' actions during his few days in Jerusalem, Judas must have reasoned, merited Jesus' arrest. On Monday, for instance, Jesus' first full day in Jerusalem, he walked from Bethany to Jerusalem and interrupted the sacrificial system at the Jewish temple by turning over the tables of the money changers and those selling doves for sacrifices. This highly subversive act illuminated what Jesus' parables outside Jerusalem had only dimly suggested. Jesus planned an outright assault on the ungodly practices associated with the very heart of the Jewish nation. Jesus' action quickly came to the attention of the authority figures, who kept an eye on him for the rest of the week. By association, Jesus' companions, the Twelve—Judas included—would have come under suspicion as well. We can well imagine Judas questioning Jesus' actions and resenting the fallout for his reputation.

On Tuesday morning, Jesus took the disciples once again to the temple and there candidly alienated the entire Jewish establishment through a series of parables and teachings. This alienation encompassed all the major players in the Jewish world: Pharisees, Herodians, Sadducees, and scribes. The only group Jesus did not condemn was represented by the poor widow, the one who contributed her penny to the treasury, and would have been immediately forgotten if it was noticed by anyone else in the first place. On the way back to Bethany for the night after a long and self-indicting day—one that sealed his fate as one who would incur the death penalty—Jesus rested on the Mount of Olives with his disciples. Looking down on the nearby temple, he predicted the destruction of this national religious and political icon.

Judas knew what was coming.

By Wednesday evening, at which time the woman poured her perfume on Jesus, Judas had probably made up his mind to cut his losses while there was still time. The Jews would celebrate

Passover the following evening, and Judas may have reasoned that he had to do something before the end of the week to get out while he still could. If Jesus predicted that his own death and the destruction of the temple were both imminent, then Judas may well have reasoned that the two events were linked with the Passover celebration. What would Jesus do to destroy both himself and the city of Jerusalem? As the end of week drew near, he didn't have much time left to bail before finding out.

As is well-known, Judas left the Passover feast, held on Thursday evening, early. The other disciples were clueless about Judas's duplicity. Only Jesus was aware of Judas's impending betrayal. Perhaps Judas had privately confronted Jesus while in Jerusalem or Bethany, just as Peter had done so publicly in Caesarea Philippi. Whatever the case, the public conversation between Jesus and Judas the night before at Simon the leper's in Bethany went over everyone's head. The same thing happened during the Last Supper. We might even be led to conclude that Jesus and Judas were speaking another language—one the other disciples did not understand—were it not for the fact that the disciples registered confusion at Jesus' cryptic remarks, which he spoke publicly, though he intended them only for Judas: "What you are about to do, do quickly" (John 13:27).

KISSING OUR PLANS GOOD-BYE
When Your Will Collides with God's

At this point in the story, we might wish to see Judas take the other available option when God does not follow our plans: to rethink the plans and adjust accordingly. This what separates followers from unfollowers. Faithful disciples of Jesus put their plans at the feet of their master. Unfollowers, like Judas here, eventually bail on Jesus when it becomes apparent that Jesus' plan differs from their own. And unlike the story of Jonah, for instance, who initially disobeyed God but repented and became restored to God before things got out of hand, the story of Judas comes to a chilling end. There is no apparent confession of guilt, though there is sorrow.

What Judas was going to do, he did it quickly.

Judas had astutely perceived that the authorities were intent on capturing and killing Jesus. This "Messiah" was just too dangerous. The trouble was, of course, that the Jewish authorities did not want to inadvertently incite a rebellion of the masses who were enamored with Jesus as a tragic hero. Judas craftily hatched a scheme to deliver his rabbi to the Jewish authorities.

We all have motives for the things we do. And Judas must have had a motive for his betrayal of Jesus. Although money may have been a contributing factor, it was not the primary reason. Judas may have been a pilferer, as the gospel of John suggests, but the fact that he returned the blood money he initially received from the Jewish leaders indicates that greed was not all that motivated Judas.

Whatever animated him, the gospel accounts make it clear that Judas did not readjust his course. At best, Judas found Jesus genuinely perplexing and completely misunderstood how Jesus' plans could be better than his own. At worst, Judas was so blinded by his plans and so desperate to secure a future for himself that he was willing to take part in a complex murder scheme. At the root of Judas's betrayal is a mind that had become fixed on a particular kind of messiah who would lead him to a prosperous future. Perhaps he felt betrayed by Jesus. He could not believe in a Suffering Servant who bore the sins of others and laid down his life to conquer death. If we're honest with ourselves, such things are not easily believed today for that matter. Who wins through self-sacrifice? Who would want to trade in his or her own plans for a prosperous future and submit to a God-King's new plan where the first shall be last, the last shall be first, and suffering is a certainty?

Judas couldn't let go of his plans because he could not imagine any other way forward.

Waving the White Flag

The story of Judas stands in stark contrast to Peter who said to Jesus, "Lord, to whom shall we go? You have the words of eternal life" (John 6:68). Judas wasn't about to let go of his life plans quite so easily. He had a plan B in mind: get some money to start over and win over the good will of Israel's puppet leaders. He wasn't all that interested in the words of eternal life if those words didn't mention the overthrow of Rome and the return of the Messiah to the land of Israel.

If Peter embodied the ideal childlike faith that rested completely on his future with Jesus, Judas trusted in himself and his own plans. I don't know about you, but I have a hard time just saying, "Wherever I end up is quite alright as long as I'm with you Jesus!" That's the ideal we should be striving for, but how many times do we attach conditions? "I'll follow you, but I also really want to get that promotion at work." "I'll follow you, but I want to live in a big renovated farm house someday." "I'll follow you, but I want to never worry about having enough money."

Peter didn't have a plan outside of asking Jesus what he should do next. Judas waited to see whether Jesus would provide what he wanted. If Jesus didn't deliver, he was ready to split. While I'm not personally invested in the liberation of an oppressed country like Judas, I can at least relate to his tendency to try to cram God into his own plans. And keep in mind, Judas was not unusual for his times. He was well within the cultural current. Just about everyone in Israel wanted exactly what he wanted. Judas was unique in that he had been hoping to find the deliverance of Israel from Rome at the hands of Jesus.

Plans come in between us and God slowly, almost imperceptibly sometimes. There was a time in my life when I didn't want to live in a city, and I resisted the possibility that God could ever use me as a writer. I resisted the possibility that I could ever offer anything of value to my poorer neighbors. In fact, I spent more time fearing that my neighbors would mug me rather than thinking of ways to help them. In each situation, I wanted to follow Jesus, but I always kept backup plans stashed away. I had goals I wanted to meet, assuming that I could keep them along with my relationship with Jesus. If I was honest, I would have said, "Well, I sure would like you to be in my life Jesus, but I also have some other great stuff that offers meaning and fulfillment. In fact, I'd like your help with some of those things."

I've observed that God sometimes calls us to make radical changes to our lives, but God also asks us to be fully present in our day-to-day lives. That means we're fully present to worship and pray. We're fully present with a spouse, children, or close friends. We're committed to the work God has given us. We take care of the possessions entrusted to us and use them well for the kingdom.

TRAITORS RARELY PLAN AHEAD

No one plans to turn his or her back on God or country. Josephus started his life as a devout Jew among either the priests or Pharisees. He even negotiated the release of Jewish priests from imprisonment under Nero. By the same token, Judas was most likely a devout Jew who never would have considered joining a murder conspiracy. They each had to make decisions about their loyalties. For Josephus, it was self-preservation. For Judas, it was a vision of Israel liberated by a certain kind of messiah. Their actions directly resulted from their personal commitments.

It's uncomfortable to think about the ways my daily schedule has revealed my commitments over the years. There once was a time when I would come home from work and watch a sports game for the entire evening and then confess in church the following Sunday, "I don't have time to pray." If I was struggling to pray, then it's no wonder why I also struggled to surrender my plans to God—I could only think of what I wanted because I wasn't on the same page with God.

None of us want to neglect the will of Jesus or betray the kingdom of God. Our visions of the kingdom become skewed or distracted gradually over time as we hold on to our plans. Sometimes this shift goes almost completely unnoticed. We might never commit an act of treachery quite like Judas or Josephus, but we certainly know how to put our own interests first.

◼7 THE JUDEANS

A MESSIAH WHO AFFIRMS MY THEOLOGY

If you're a student of the Bible who believes that the stories recorded are factually accurate, then you're most likely not a fan of theologian Friedrich Schleiermacher. If you haven't heard of him, then you've probably heard of his work. Simply put, Schleiermacher denied the historical truthfulness of certain parts of the Bible. According to this German theologian, the Bible exists to give us a spiritual encounter with God. Therefore, the recording of factual events is less important since these do not necessarily connect us with God.

Schleiermacher's leading critic in the United States was Charles Hodge at Princeton Seminary. Hodge was a conservative Christian legend known for his dedication to teaching the historically factual nature of the Bible, prolific writing, and gentle disposition. Hodge saw Schleiermacher's denial of certain parts of Scripture as a significant departure from historic Christianity. Roughly a hundred years later, Christian theologian Karl Barth would level a similar critique of Schleiermacher.

Writing about Hodge and Schleiermacher for the Christian Vision Project, Richard Mouw, the former president at Fuller Theological Seminary, wrote that Hodge added a notable caveat in his critique of Schleiermacher. In fact, Hodge's systematic theology text included a footnote about Schleiermacher:

> During his studies in Germany, Hodge reported, he had frequently attended services at Schleiermacher's church and had been impressed that the hymns sung there "were always evangelical and spiritual in an eminent degree, filled with praise and gratitude to our Redeemer." He went on to note that he had been told by one of Schleiermacher's colleagues that often, in the evenings, the theologian would call his family together, saying: "Hush, children; let us sing a hymn of praise to Christ." And then Hodge adds this tribute to Schleiermacher: "Can we doubt that he is singing those praises now? To whomever Christ is God, St. John assures us, Christ is a Saviour."[1]

Schleiermacher would certainly never be confused with a conservative North American Christian. However, two leading evangelical theologians who have credentials above reproach held back their judgment on the man who led the attack on the historic truthfulness of the Bible. While strongly disagreeing with Schleiermacher's theology, they also appreciated his sincere love for God. Hodge and Mouw chose the refreshingly Christlike approach to let God do the judging, even if they pointed out the flaws in Schleiermacher's approach to God. They could see that God was doing something with their theological opponent, even if his teachings departed dramatically from historic Christianity.

The best Christian theologians understand that theology isn't the same as devotion to God or the experience of God. When God shows up, it's not our place to limit God or to tell him who he can save or how he should work. Perhaps our theology and rules can even prevent us from seeing what God wants to do among us today. While we have good reasons for holding to the historic truthfulness of the Bible, perhaps we need to learn to see God at work in the people we're most likely to rule out.

WHAT GOD CANNOT DO

Setting the Scene

Very few of us have done the same exact thing every day for thirty-eight years. Even if you've worked at a job for that length of time, you took vacations and enjoyed regular weekends. A crippled or blind person in the days of Jesus had only one way to survive each day: beg. If you're going to beg, then you'll need to stake out the spot with the most people. In a city like Jerusalem, which didn't have any natural bodies of water nearby, the pool of Bethesda (which was technically two pools in close proximity to one another) offered an ideal place to beg because it was a large spring where many gathered. It was also probably close to a gate entering the city. Such a location could be especially helpful for a beggar during a Jewish festival when the population of Jerusalem swelled by the thousands.

Something about this man stood out to Jesus and his company as they walked to the pool. Perhaps someone remarked how this same man had been doing the same exact thing for thirty-eight years near this pool just outside the temple mount in Jerusalem. They may have seen him every year since their childhood when they visited Jerusalem for the festivals and holy days. We also learn the curious detail that this man held loosely to a local superstition that an angel would occasionally stir the waters in the pool and cause the first person in to be healed. Such beliefs were common in the ancient world, just as they still are in many other parts of the world today. Whether or not the man begging truly believed this could happen or he just used it as his excuse for begging at such a popular public location, we at least know that there was something about him that caused people to take notice of him and point him out to Jesus. His life would never be the same—or at least it didn't have to be.

Giving God a Break

Besides Jesus and the lame man, the other main characters in this story are the "Jews" (see John 5). Although "Jews" is the literal translation, it's most likely that John meant the Judeans around Jerusalem, as opposed to the Jews in Galilee and other regions outside of Judea. Some translations such as the NIV go as far as suggesting that they were the "Jewish leaders" (John 5:10) who interacted with Jesus. Part of our challenge here is determining the range of public opinion about Jesus among the Jews in Judea. There clearly were many in Judea who supported him without necessarily becoming committed disciples. Jesus was popular enough that the Sanhedrin feared a riot if they killed him. However, we can see that each visit to Jerusalem brought about a fair share of controversy with the Jewish leaders, and we can assume there was a large contingent of local Judeans both inside and outside Jerusalem who opposed Jesus. If they didn't have their own misgivings about Jesus, then they at least refused to stand against their religious leaders.

While the elite teachers of the law, the Pharisees, and the conservative Jewish political leaders connected to the temple, the Sadducees, led the charge in plotting Jesus' death, a passage like this suggests that there were common Jews in Judea who also resented this upstart preacher and his band of followers from a backwater place like Galilee. It's possible that particularly strong regional affinities contributed to the tension between Jesus and the Judeans in this passage. As we discuss this passage further, we'll refer to the opposition as "Judeans" with the caveat that some Judeans supported Jesus and it's likely that some even became his followers.

The Judeans in this story opposed Jesus because of the way he spoke about himself, the law, and the traditional customs that had come to define proper observance of the law. In fact, healing on the Sabbath resulted in some of his sharpest confrontations. The fourth commandment states, "Remember the Sabbath day by keeping it holy" (Ex. 20:8). The rabbis defined the terms *remembering* and *keeping holy* through a series of traditions such as limiting travel and not permitting cooking on the Sabbath. At the very least, carrying a mat on the Sabbath was clearly off limits. The Judeans would have thought of the prophet Jeremiah who wrote, "This is what the LORD says: Be careful not to carry a load on the Sabbath day or bring it through the gates of Jerusalem. Do not bring a load out of your houses or do any work on the Sabbath, but keep the Sabbath day holy, as I commanded your ancestors" (Jer. 17:21–22). (Another more substantive interpretation of how to honor and not violate the fourth commandment comes from the Mishnah in tractate *Sabbath* 7:2, which forbids the carrying of things from one place to another on the Sabbath. The carrying of beds is specifically forbidden in tractate 10:5.)

It's hard for us to imagine how important the Sabbath became for Jews. It wasn't just an identity marker that set them apart from their pagan enemies; it also created space to rest and, most importantly, to worship. Publicly challenging the accepted teachings on the Sabbath—during a religious festival no less—caused quite a stir in the community because it essentially denied one's reverence for God and identity as part of his chosen people. When Jesus began to challenge the Sabbath, he wasn't just making a statement about worship; he was challenging the people's notions about what mattered most to God. Jesus pointed them to something other than getting all of the details right—a significant theological shift that many were not ready to accept.

What Jesus Did

In the midst of messianic expectations and a culture that rigidly obeyed the Sabbath, Jesus confronted the crippled man at the pool of Bethesda with a startling question. "Do you want to get well?" (John 5:6). After thirty-eight years of begging as a cripple, it's possible that this man had resigned himself to his lot. Could he even imagine a life other than the one he had? Even though he had a miracle worker in front of him, he only mentioned the local superstition of an angel stirring the waters to heal the first person who entered. He was far from believing in the power of God. Perhaps he didn't know anything about Jesus, but it's more likely that he didn't think the Messiah would want anything to do with a cripple.

Whatever the lame man thought to himself, Jesus made the startling statement, "Pick up your mat and walk" (John 5:8). With that command, Jesus took two controversial actions on the Sabbath in the eyes of the observant Judeans around him: He healed a man, and he commanded the man to violate the Sabbath by carrying his mat. There's no doubt that Jesus used this moment to call the theology of the Judeans into question. Would they miss out on the good works of God for the sake of following their interpretation of the Sabbath?

When Jesus told the Pharisees on another occasion that the Sabbath was made for people, not people for the Sabbath (Mark 2:27), he challenged their fundamental assumptions about how to interpret the law and about the role of the Sabbath in particular. This scene picks up on similar themes. God's plan for the law was to provide a way for his people to love and worship him as well as to provide standards for justice and mercy in their dealings with one another. The purpose of the law had always been to give life. The law itself was meant to renew God's people, not to constrict their lives. God wasn't concerned with how perfectly his people kept the Sabbath. Rather, the concern was that the Sabbath should be kept holy and set apart for worship and rest.

According to Jesus, the key question related to the Sabbath wasn't, "Am I resting properly?" Jesus wanted them to ask, "Am I taking part in the new life that comes from God?" Part of receiving God's new life is taking time to rest and worship, but the means, observing a holy day of rest, had become the goal rather than using the Sabbath to meet with God and to experience his life. All of their rules and interpretations of Scripture prevented them from experiencing the holiness of God—which was the entire point of the Sabbath in the first place!

Jesus was clearly disgusted with the way the Judeans had turned the Sabbath into a system of rules to follow, so perhaps we can understand the approach he took in this scene. By healing the man and then commanding him to carry his mat home, he provoked the Judeans, pushing them to choose what is most important. Would they rejoice over the man's healing, or would they quibble over the details of observing the Sabbath?

As we may expect, the Judeans immediately called out the man for violating the Sabbath. Perhaps we're shocked that they didn't recognize the miracle of this well-known, long-time cripple walking down the street in the first place. However, there wasn't just a high level of theological pressure to condemn the man and Jesus. The Judeans also had the pressure of their community and their religious establishment. There was only one appropriate response to this man and Jesus if they wanted to belong to their community. Whether it was from communal pressure to toe the theological line or their personally strict theology, the Judeans missed out on the work of God among them and condemned a man who should have been celebrated. This turn of events was the last thing the lame man would have expected.

Instead of enjoying the blessing of this miracle, the healed man faced opposition from his community. It must have been shocking to move from the margins of society to the center of attention—the center of unwanted attention at that. He responded as anyone in his place would: "It's not my fault." By blaming Jesus he redirected the attention of the leaders away from himself while still giving himself a shot to belong in his own community.

We should remember that Jesus wasn't from Judea. This man would have to rebuild his life in this community after Jesus returned to Galilee when the festival ended. The last thing he wanted was a confrontation with the observant Jews. He had spent his entire life on the margins, and now that he could finally participate in the Jewish community, he wasn't about to give up this opportunity.

Before leaving the man, Jesus offered a chilling rebuke, "Stop sinning or something worse may happen to you" (John 5:14). We don't know for sure what Jesus had in mind. Could there be some occasional afflictions that God brings as a punishment for a particular sin? While Jesus clearly stated that bad things in life were not the direct result of sin (Luke 13:1–5), he wanted this man to know that the disapproval of the Judeans was the least of his worries. Perhaps he only meant that this man would be in danger of hell if he continued on his current course. Perhaps he meant that something physically bad could befall him. It's most likely that Jesus offered him a striking lesson in perspective by challenging his lack of fear of God. The worst this man could imagine was being crippled or being excluded from his community by the religious leaders. Jesus warned this man that his fears were misplaced. If he lived to win over the approval of his Judean neighbors, he would forfeit the mercy that Jesus had shown him.

Would God Violate the Sabbath?

Looming in the background of this story is a larger conflict between Jesus and the religious leaders in Jerusalem. It wasn't that they just disagreed on theological points surrounding the rules for obeying the Sabbath. They disagreed about the very nature of God and therefore the basis for Jesus' authority.

Jesus understood himself as one with the Father, which, to the religious leaders, conflicted with the verse: "The LORD our God, the LORD is one" (Deut. 6:4). To suggest that God could be Father, Son, and Spirit seemed to run counter to the absolute fundamentals of Judaism. Jesus' referral to himself as one with God was a shocking revelation that confounded his listeners, but the Judeans who met Jesus had a confusing matter to sort out on their own. Why would this man standing among them claim the authority of God and the power to redefine the Sabbath among other customs and laws? The Judeans didn't just get the Sabbath wrong; they had a completely wrong picture of God.

Jesus stated that he performed this miracle because God also worked on the Sabbath. While it wasn't unheard of for the Jewish rabbis of this time to puzzle over the sovereignty of God and the observance of the Sabbath, it was completely new to think of God coming to earth as a common man, let alone for God to suggest a different understanding of the Sabbath. Just as the Pharisees were confounded at Jesus' statement that a house divided could not stand, so the Judeans could not fathom how God was divided against himself by simultaneously being for and against the Sabbath.

Naturally, Jesus' provocative statement infuriated the Jewish authorities. In their minds, shaped as they were by the Hebrew Bible and the traditional interpretation of certain passages, Jesus could not *be* God since he was a poor man from an insignificant town and untrained in the law, among other things, and Jesus could not be *from* God since he clearly violated the Sabbath, which demonstrated that he was not from God, let alone actually God.

Jesus demonstrated the limits of theology in this encounter. For all that the Judeans could imagine about God, they simply couldn't grasp a God who would show up like Jesus. It is worthwhile to dedicate time to pondering the mysteries of God and to order our lives around obediently following the teachings of Scripture, but even these good practices can cloud the reality of God himself. Observing the law and traditions became its own kind of idolatry. The Judeans found out that the "god" they worshiped didn't necessarily match the true God walking among. Rather than affirming everything the Judeans believed and practiced, Jesus asked them to rethink their most basic beliefs about God and what God wanted from them.

WHEN DOES THEOLOGY GET IN THE WAY?
Balancing Theology's Details with Mercy

We want to get our theology right because it matters. It matters that Jesus is fully the Son of God and that he became fully human. It matters that Jesus physically rose from the dead and promised to return. It matters that Jesus performed miracles, cast out demons, and performed a host of other actions that illustrated the arrival of God's kingdom before sending down the Holy Spirit at Pentecost. These are the basics of the Christian faith that make it distinct and set it apart. Depending on one's theological tradition, we will all most likely add to this list, or some Christians might attempt to shorten the list. Once we move beyond the essentials of our faith, the opportunities for theological debates are endless, since the Bible is an ancient book set in a variety of different cultures and diverse historical contexts. We're going to disagree about how we spend money, how marriages function, how singles date, how pastors lead, and how churches serve. Some of us ground our identity in particular theological beliefs, making it hard to hear what others say to us.

How do we balance mercy and attentiveness to others with the need to believe and practice Christianity to the best of our understanding?

There are any number of directions we can go here, but here's one suggestion: Can we use our imaginations to ask What-if questions? In other words, the Judeans could have asked, "what if God wanted to heal someone on the Sabbath?" or "What if God showed up in a human body?" These were dangerous questions that upset the status quo, let alone the accepted theology of their day. However, the Judeans' outright dismissal of Jesus could have turned into an opportunity for greater dialogue and even acceptance of Jesus if they'd been willing to entertain views outside of their own.

It's not common today for us to entertain opposing viewpoints. We have news channels that spin the news in whatever direction we like, seminaries that produce pastors with very specific theologies that conform to our own, and churches that can spend more time addressing the faults of other Christians rather than dealing with their own issues. It's always easier to affirm our own beliefs by picking apart what others affirm or to try to win over converts from another theological tradition. Hearing the beliefs of someone else can seem dangerous. Isn't there a risk of being "corrupted" by that person's theology?

Jesus provocatively insinuated in this story that fear and defensiveness surrounding a person's belief system indicates that we may have some major problems and our beliefs are not as secure as we'd imagined. If a conversation with someone who disagrees with us can truly unsettle all that we've shaped our lives around, then perhaps we're trusting in the wrong things.

This story shoves us away from the uncertain rules and beliefs that can't support us in favor of resting primarily on God alone.

Jesus wanted his listeners to stop relying on Sabbath rules. They needed to see that God was in their midst—a God who was able to heal and rise from the dead, even on the Sabbath. The Judeans thought they found life, but they were looking in the wrong place. Their inability to imagine anything different kept them from experiencing the healing touch of God.

Finding God in the Sabbath

Back in the 1960s, many American Christians had a different approach to the Sabbath than we do today. Many wouldn't go shopping, lest they require someone else to "sin" by working on the Sabbath. States passed blue laws that forbid the sale of alcohol. Some families wouldn't even engage in recreational activities like swimming in the summer or playing sports on Sunday. I heard one story from a family friend that illustrates this: A non-Christian friend of his had joined his family for a vacation at a cabin by a lake. On a particularly hot and steamy Sunday, everyone sat around talking. No one was allowed to go swimming because of the Sabbath. This non-Christian friend had enough sitting around and sweating while a perfectly cool and inviting body of water stood by. If he was going to sit anywhere, it was going to be in the water. So he took a lawn chair, put it in a shallow part of the lake, and sat down. Although he was wet and in the lake, he was not technically violating the Sabbath because he was not "swimming."

We find stories like this amusing, but they force us to ask tough questions about how we're supposed to interpret the Bible today. There is something to be said for resting, worshiping, and reading Scripture on a Sunday. These are all good things. I can think of many parents with children who would love someone to command them to sit around all day and quietly reflect on God!

In this passage, we see the danger of turning Christianity into a series of rules we have to obey. Blindly following rules cannot only deprive us from the joy of knowing God, but also limit our ability to see God at work in the people around us. The Judeans let their Sabbath rules come between themselves and Jesus—to say nothing about those they alienated and attacked over their Sabbath observance differences. In fact, it's fascinating to think that Jesus said very little about actually keeping the Sabbath holy. It wasn't a concern for him. His mission had more to do with helping people meet the Father and live in his kingdom than with making a rule into a weapon.

Perhaps we're uncomfortable thinking that Jesus left religious observance so wide open and unanswered. Doesn't the Old Testament still apply in some way to Christians? Or do we risk missing the significance of Jesus if we fail to see the Sabbath rest from God that he brought? The problem we face in any religion is majoring on minor points and thereby neglecting what is most important. We could observe a perfectly restful Sunday, but we could fail to offer peace and restoration to our friends and neighbors. We could avoid work all day Sunday, but we could spend every day trying to appease God or to atone for sins that have long been forgiven. If we neglect the rest God gives, then it doesn't matter what we do on Sunday.

We can all get this right on a theology test, but it's tough to sort out the practices of going through the motions and those that help us actively meet with God. It's quite possible for two people to have the same rules and routines on a given Sunday, but their reasons for following them and their relationships with God the Father can be completely different.

The Cost of Theology and Community

Before we criticize the Judeans or the lame man too harshly in this chapter's story, we would do well to remember the communal aspects of theology. We learn how to read, interpret, and apply the Bible in church communities, and those churches are within denominations that help define our identities and provide some of our closest friends. Deviating from the accepted theology of a group can prove costly and isolating depending on the way each group values a particular understanding of the Bible. Even those who have misgivings about a church's theology may still feel pressured to conform for the sake of keeping the peace.

Perhaps this tension between theology and community is no sharper in North American churches than in relation to homosexuality. There are those in churches who can't imagine Christians not welcoming homosexuals, and others who can't imagine not quickly quoting passages like 1 Corinthians 6:9 with any homosexuals they encounter. And then there are the younger Christians who are divided in their interpretations of the Bible concerning homosexuality but who generally aren't invested in fighting against same-sex marriage. In churches where this issue causes tension and division, we can see the role that community plays in our theology. There may be Christians on either end of this issue who feel unable to voice their true convictions because they fear being labeled a bigot or heretic.

Lost in these debates are the bigger issues in Scripture: loving our neighbors and identifying the root sins that can destroy our faith, such as pride, lust, and greed. Classifying homosexuality as the worst sin a person can commit has become a test of one's theology and view of Scripture. As a result, we've lost sight of what God may be doing in the people on both sides of the debate.

While convictions are important, we can run the risk of using theology to label and then dismiss people out of hand.

Loving the Bible, Missing the Point

Some today may become uneasy with the implications of Jesus' teaching and actions in this passage. He clearly asked the Judeans to think beyond the specific commands of the law to discern its true intentions and goals. Such thinking moves beyond black-and-white rules or categories and into a far more challenging place where we have some boundaries, but not as many as we think. The Sabbath should be kept holy, but the "how" of this holiness is far from clear.

Let's begin with a confession: We all like clear, simple rules and doctrines we can follow and believe. Scripture gives us some points that are simple enough to grasp. The two greatest commands are to love God and love others. However, there are plenty of other points where we can't sort out the details today. To what extent can our attention to theology keep us from the ultimate goals of loving God and loving others?

There is much at stake here. We could end up badly misrepresenting God and missing out on God's blessings for ourselves, to say nothing of alienating the very people who need the good news most. Remember, it's tragic that the Judeans missed out on the works of Jesus, but it's just as bad that they condemned this man who had just been healed. They appear foolish and petty to us today, but have we failed to see the greater works of God in our own day because we have become fixated on a particular theological point?

Depending on where you go to church, you will be taught to focus on personal holiness, the sovereignty of God, miraculous signs, or the justice of God here on earth. We all have our points of emphasis that shape how we approach God, relate to others, and read the Bible. We've all learned to zero in on specific parts of the Bible that resonate with our backgrounds. Lost in the mix may be points in Scripture that don't quite line up with what we expect to find. Just by traveling to another country, we are able to detect that each Christian culture focuses on different aspects of the Bible.

As often as Jesus spoke about wisely using money, there are far more verses in the Bible about God's concern for the poor. Americans will eagerly buy books about responsible money management. This, of course, is not necessarily a bad thing, but many of us struggle to figure out what it means to clothe the naked, feed the hungry, or visit the prisoner. I know how to open a savings account, but it's quite another matter to block off time in my schedule to visit inmates or to make a meal for the local community center. I find it far easier to define obedient discipleship in terms of what is most natural and easy for me. In fact, I can come up with great excuses for not caring for the poor and imprisoned. Aren't they irresponsible and lazy? Aren't they getting what they deserve? Shouldn't we focus on giving them the gospel message and not "waste" our time on physical needs or social justice?

We're all naturally going to be drawn to the less-disruptive parts of the Bible and the parts that are less demanding on us. In fact, Israel historically had no problem maintaining a sacrificial system or celebrating holy festivals. Anyone could wear the right robe, cut his hair the right way, or get circumcised. It was far more difficult to support God's kind of justice for their neighbors. Politicians and judges took bribes, the wealthy made "sound business decisions" by paying low wages to the poor, and everyone believed that simply "owning" the temple made them safe. Would God ever abandon the people who kept his law and maintained his temple? Exile and years of Roman rule suggested that they'd made some tragic theological errors about what matters most to God.

We all do this.

In Matthew 25, Jesus warned his disciples that many will find themselves outside God's kingdom because they neglected to care for the hungry, sick, homeless, and imprisoned. We could downplay this by talking about good stewardship or reaching the lost in our communities. We could take away the force of Jesus' command and say, "I've been justified because I believe Jesus died for me." However, if we claim the presence of Christ in our lives, shouldn't our desires and actions resemble his own? Why do we have to search for ways to dance around a passage like this? It's possible that we can use the Bible to undermine its more important messages. We can fail to use the Bible to connect with the heart of the Father and the life of the Spirit when we get weighed down with our own priorities or the minor details.

TRUE STORIES THAT MATTER

We hold on to these stories in Scripture because they are true, but affirming them or learning about them isn't where our responsibilities end. These stories are historically true and they're supposed to change us by helping us encounter God. The former is what the Judeans got right; the latter is what theologians like Friedrich Schleiermacher got right. Ignoring the truth or the uncomfortable relevance of Scripture will cause problems with our theology and how we relate to God and one another.

We all want to be on God's side. We all think we have the right theology. We base major decisions on our beliefs and how we interpret the Bible. Our beliefs impact the kind of work we do, where we go to school, who we marry, what kind of marriage we have, and who our friends are. With so much invested in our theology, it's hard to think we've made a mistake. The costs could be significant if we change something about our practices or beliefs.

Sometimes God will be working among people and in places that make us uncomfortable and even cause us to second-guess those beliefs and practices we believe are central to our identity. No matter how hard we try to let Scripture guide our lives, there's always a chance that we have some part of our theology wrong. A mistake like that could cause us to miss out on the work of God among us and alienate those who need our support the most.

NOTE

1. Richard Mouw, "An Open-Handed Gospel," *Christianity Today*, The Christian Vision Project, April 8, 2008, http://www.christianvisionproject.com/2008/04/an_openhanded_gospel.html.

■8 HEROD AND PILATE

A MESSIAH WHO CATERS TO THE POWERFUL

Martin Luther and the Protestant Reformation would have never lasted long if it hadn't been for the Turks. When Luther protested the abuses of the Catholic Church, the pope had designs to send the French into Germany to suppress the rebellious monk and his followers. Many people fled France to avoid persecution and even death at the hands of their Catholic rulers. The German princes had military forces of their own, but not nearly the same strength as the French army. Luckily for Luther and the German people, they represented the lesser of two evils in the eyes of the French. With the Turkish army invading Europe, the besieged city of Vienna represented a last hope to protect "Christian Europe."

With the future of Europe hanging in the balance, the pope had to back off his plans to overthrow the German princes and kill Luther. The German and French armies marched to battle the Turks outside Vienna. With the combined armies of Europe working together, Vienna survived the siege and the Turks retreated. Although Luther and his fellow Protestants avoided the most potent threat to their movement, difficult days still stretched ahead.

Assassins regularly plotted to take Luther's life, and he was only saved through the cunning and power of German princes who viewed him as a valuable political asset. Luther spent a great deal of time under the protection of a German prince who gave him the safety he needed to translate the Bible into German, a welcome alternative for the common people since before that the Bible had only been translated into Latin.

Luther was no stranger to the upsides and downsides of power. The future of his work seemingly hinged on the decisions made in castles and back rooms about who to invade and which ally made the most sense to retain. He was surrounded by rulers who lived and died by swords and political cunning. If anyone in the church was positioned to understand the costs, challenges, and downfalls of power, it was Martin Luther.

In Luther's last sermon, which he preached just a few days before dying in his hometown of Eisleben, Germany, he returned to a theme that was especially dear to him in his later years: God's power cloaked in weakness. For Luther, God revels in paradox and loves to turn the tables on what the world assumes about wisdom, truth, justice, love, and strength. As Luther saw abuses of power firsthand in both church and government, he felt the implications of Scripture particularly acutely. Although

Luther died just days after preaching on this favorite topic of his, his writings speak boldly and often about the God of the Bible who veils his power in weakness.

In the eyes of Luther, God doesn't make exceptions. If God manifests his power through weakness and powerlessness rather than brute strength and pride, we are expected to do the same.

There are no two moments in the life of Jesus the Messiah more indicative of God's power through weakness than his birth and death. Indeed, these two events serve as sturdy bookmarks that enclose the story of the Messiah. Together they boldly demonstrate that God does not abuse power or cater to the powerful. If anything, he exposes their flaws and offers a striking alternative.

At either end of these bookmarks in the gospel accounts stand the counter-messiahs or historical impostors of Jesus the Christ: Herod the Great and Pontius Pilate. Their perspectives concerning power could not have been further from Jesus', as Jesus would himself later say to Pilate before his death by crucifixion, "My kingdom is not of this world" (John 18:36).

We're so far removed from the time of Jesus that it's hard to relate to the political realities of his time. The Jews wrapped up their religious and national hopes in one messianic leader. Meanwhile, the Romans had been deeply divided just before the time of Christ over the rule of the senate as opposed to a single emperor—a "Caesar." When Caesar solidified his rule, he also adopted the title "son of God" for good measure. If every political movement thinks that God is on their side, the only way to one-up them is by declaring yourself a god. Jesus stepped into a world of kings, emperors, and false gods and then declared himself a king, but not a king who resembled his contemporaries.

Before we can gain a firm grasp on the kind of kingdom Jesus brought and what it could mean for us today, let's look at two people who provided foils to the kingdom Jesus brought.

AN UPSIDE-DOWN WORLD AND A RIGHT-SIDE-UP GOD

If you lived during the days of Herod the Great, the first word that came to mind when you thought of him would not be *great*. Paranoid, bloodthirsty, and manipulative, Herod killed anyone from Jewish peasants to his own wives and family members, including three sons and several brothers-in-law. Obsessed with building palaces and cities, he left his mark all over the land of Jerusalem. You can still walk around his enormous swimming pool near Jericho where he also drowned a number of officials. His fortresses near Bethlehem and the Dead Sea were both powerful strongholds and beautifully decorated. As if that wasn't enough, he built Caesarea from scratch. Of course, to do all of this, he had to tax the people of Israel into further poverty and used a heavy hand to kill anyone suspected of insurrection. He was so hated that he ordered a large number of Jewish prisoners to be killed on the day of his own death to ensure there would be mourning in the land. No one carried out that order.

At the time of Jesus' birth in Bethlehem, Herod was an old man, and since his kingdom would soon pass to another, perhaps he was on heightened alert for any hint of rebellion. The transfer of kingship was always an ideal time to test the loyalties of a royal court. After Mary gave birth to Jesus in a lowly manger and cared for him in the humble village of Bethlehem, Herod flew into a rage when a party of wise men arrived from a distant land in search of the newborn king of the Jews. If he wasn't already paranoid, Herod now had a contender to the throne to worry about. He'd worked too hard to maintain control of his kingdom to give it up to a Jewish insurgent.

In a politically stable Western nation like America, it's hard for us to imagine just how much Herod had at stake. He wasn't elected king. He didn't enjoy popular support. The entire political process in the land of Israel before him was a chaotic mess that moved from warring Jewish kings to warring Roman puppet kings. Herod established his kingdom through military victories, appeasing his political opponents, converting to Judaism, and marrying into a Jewish royal family in an attempt to legitimize his rule. He had played the political game masterfully and had used force frequently and with deadly effect.

Herod's conception of power had everything to do with his ability to force anyone to bend to his will. By setting up a hierarchy of power, he used his place at the top to accomplish his will and to keep his opponents at bay. Herod wasn't interested in sharing power or giving it away, so we can only imagine his rage at learning about a newborn king of the Jews from the magi.

The contrast of the two kings is stunning: Jesus was born in the tiny village of Bethlehem, where probably only a few hundred people lived. And right next to Bethlehem, Herod had constructed a gigantic fortress of dirt and earth called Herodion, overlooking the tiny village he almost totally crushed. Whereas Herod had to make a giant mount to provide a fortress for himself, God allowed his Son, the infant King, to be vulnerably born in a feeding trough in Roman-occupied territory. As a harmless child emerged in the world to bring peace and drive out fear, a paranoid tyrant used fear and brute force as he viciously fought to hang onto power until his dying breath. We can well appreciate the "success" of

Herod the Great since his sons who followed him ultimately struggled to manage the volatile land of Israel after him. When Herod's sons couldn't keep the peace in Jerusalem and the surrounding area, Rome intervened and appointed their own man: a prefect named Pontius Pilate.

Pilate's Copilots

If you imagined your worst day at work, there's a good chance it can't come close to a typical day for Pontius Pilate. As Rome's appointed ruler in the unpredictable land of Israel where the threat of revolt simmered beneath the surface of every religious festival, Pilate had to juggle the demands of Rome with the daily discontent and religious zeal of his Jewish subjects. With the responsibility to collect taxes and keep the peace with a sizable Roman army at his command, Pilate regularly met with Jewish authorities who considered him unclean and wouldn't even enter his building. We can only imagine how relations between Pilate and the Jews deteriorated from that point on. To ensure peace, Pilate regularly met with Jewish client rulers like Herod Agrippa and Jewish religious leaders like Caiaphas. Until the trial of Jesus, his relationship with Agrippa had been one of mutual hostility.

Pontius Pilate was the fifth Roman prefect of Judea, from 26–36 A.D. He was replaced as prefect in 36 A.D. because he harshly put down a Samaritan revolt, a detail that helps us understand his concerns when he met Jesus. Pilate avoided the annoyances of Jerusalem by residing in the Roman colony of Caesarea Maritima on the Mediterranean coast, but he also spent considerable time in Jerusalem during important Jewish festivals like Passover. This was the most opportune time for Jewish uprisings to occur since much of the surrounding Jewish population was present. The people were especially mindful, given the liturgy of the Passover feast, of the tightening grip of the Roman occupation on their land despite God's will for them to live and worship freely.

Pilate's disdain for the Jews only heightened when the Sanhedrin asked him to kill Jesus, essentially making Pilate do their dirty work. Pilate's antagonism toward Caiaphas and the other council members was palpable when he first said, "Judge him by your own law" (John 18:31). Then, after confirming that Jesus considered himself the king of the Jews, Pilate comically declared, "I find no basis for a charge against him" (John 18:38). In the end, Pilate only complied because the Sanhedrin threatened to report him to a higher power—Caesar in Rome—who already had Pilate on his radar because of his past brutality. Pilate reasoned that killing one man suspected of treason would be preferable to dealing with an entire uprising. As a final jab at Caiaphas and the Sanhedrin, Pilate ensured that Jesus' guilty sign read, "King of the Jews."

Much like Herod, Pilate could only rule Israel by using fear, violence, and political scheming. There was a constant chess match where each side fought to gain an upper hand or to secure an obligation from someone. In the worlds of Pilate and Herod, any vulnerability could be exploited. Weakness and gentleness were invitations for rebellion.

Acting Like a King

A popular theme in books, movies, and television shows is the sudden rise to power of an average person who knows nothing of protocols or how to handle the responsibilities of a political or royal position. We expect the newcomer to learn the ropes and begin ruling according to the standards presented by a trusted advisor. If there were standards for ruling as king at the time of Jesus, they would have looked a lot like the policies of Herod and Pilate: neutralize any threat, choose the lesser of two evils, sacrifice justice today to get what you want, never let your opponents get an edge on you, and don't be afraid to get your hands dirty with a little violence and intrigue. In many ways, the rules of politics and governing haven't changed. When Jesus showed up in a lowly manger, he set into motion God's plan to provide an alternative to the rulers at the time.

While we should be careful about making a precise blueprint out of Jesus' approach to power and politics, there are several striking aspects to the way he brought the kingdom of God to the people of his day. For starters, Jesus remained completely removed from the political structures of his day. He still welcomed Roman soldiers, Roman officials, and Jewish council members to his gatherings, but we don't have any record of him petitioning politicians or running for office. We should be careful not to read too much into this. Rome took care of appointing its own officials, and John the Baptist stands as exhibit A for the results of political dissent back in that day. However, it's striking to note that besides avoiding a bloody battle with the Romans, Jesus spent his entire ministry on the margins, powerless and without title.

The trial of Jesus is ironic as the Jewish authorities and Pilate fought over who got to kill Jesus when he was the true King with power over them both. Such a scene leaves us puzzled. It's almost too much to even begin pondering what it could mean. Why would a God who is powerful enough to save his own life submit to death? Jesus' refusal to resist the authorities in power provides hints about his own approach to power. Perhaps the true use of power isn't that of death, but life. In other words, being able to kill or drive fear into people isn't true power. True power removes fear and can even raise the dead to life. Jesus' power "ruled" through service and love that won over hearts and built a kind of loyalty that kings and presidents don't understand and can't use because they need people to be expendable. Jesus ruled by making a family. Rulers like Herod and Pilate legitimized their rule and got things done through the threat and use of force. Pilate and just about everyone else only saw a weak peasant with messianic delusions. How could submitting to death make Jesus *more* powerful? How could the true king win by losing?

The presence of crosses bearing the battered bodies of insurrectionists would have been a regular sight outside of cities ruled by Romans. The cross wasn't just a way to kill someone; the cross told people that Rome had won and everyone better get in line behind Caesar and his minions unless they wanted to die on a cross as well. Jesus took the symbol of Rome's power to take away life and adopted it as his own symbol of God's power to give life.[1] Instead of a ruler like Herod killing people to take away power, Jesus ruled by dying and then using the cross and resurrection to impart life and give away power.

THE END OF POWER

Who Does God Honor?

It's easy to honor and respect a person with power. That person can make life unpleasant if you don't! As both a volunteer and staff member in several different churches, I saw how the complaints of the most influential or wealthy spurred me to take action. I was frequently tempted to disregard the feedback or complaints of those who weren't as influential or wealthy. We all know who can make our lives difficult and who can make our lives easier, and that is precisely our problem when it comes to power and influence. When we're only concerned for our own interests, it makes no sense to worry about the poor and powerless. When you want to advance your own agenda, it makes sense to turn the influential and powerful into your ideal models. They are the ones who have achieved what is most desirable for us, and critiquing them could end up as a critique of ourselves. Much of my discomfort around the powerless has to do with my own hope to appear "together" around my peers—and pretty much everyone else.

This is uncomfortable for me. I don't like to admit the extent to which appearances and money influence my judgment and personal goals. However, there's another angle to power in our lives. It's easy to see how power and wealth corrupted rulers like Pilate and Herod, but we can make a grave error when we say, "I just need a little more."

To think of the number of buildings Jesus financed in comparison with Herod, we get a glimpse of what God desires to build and what he values. Unlike Herod's vain obsession with himself, Jesus built up his followers and showed that true power is given away. The one who serves and puts him- or herself last has nothing to lose and everything to give because he or she isn't full of false hopes, empty promises, or meaningless gains. If Jesus had given his disciples earthly power, he would have given them something that they couldn't hold on to forever and that they would have had to fight to maintain. Herod and Pilate fought like literal mad men to hold onto their power. Jesus never bothered with their kind of power, so he appeared crazy to the rulers of his time. But in truth, he was the sane one. When Jesus offered his followers his body and blood at the Last Supper and then imparted his Holy Spirit, he gave them gifts that brought true life and power that would endure for eternity because they came from God and served the purpose of benefitting others. As they learned to serve, they gained a different kind of influence won through laying down their lives—influence that doesn't fear being overthrown. Such influence is life-giving to all involved and frees us to love both God and our neighbors.

As we compare the work of God to the work of humanity, the differences between the power God honors and the power that men honor are extreme. Curiously, we can use similar language for both kinds of power. Jesus and Herod were both influential and respected. The great difference is that Herod made people obey him, while Jesus loved people into obedience. Jesus was unmistakably a true servant of the people, while Herod only served people when he had his own goals in mind. Jesus' power was completely emptied of serving his own purposes so that he could build God's family, while Herod aimed only to build his own name and kingdom.

Serving others and empowering the powerless is the only way to build something that is worthwhile and lasting. As good as power and influence may feel, it won't last. It will only put us in situations where we'll be fearful and paranoid, forcing us to serve ourselves and defend our own interests ahead of others. If we desire the honor and approval that only God gives, we can begin by asking what it looks like to serve the interests of others ahead of our own.

If Only I Had More Influence

I have a tendency to offer excuses for not doing things that are good for me and others. I've told myself, "I'll donate more to charity when we earn more money," or, "I'll do more for the poor when I have more influence." My thinking ties obedience to God with position and wealth. Jesus launched what we could call an "insurgent" ministry on the margins with very few resources. In fact, the key to his ministry was the power of God, not a large tribe of followers, a robust bank account, or an attractive facility. We often lie to ourselves that we need more stuff or more influence to minister to others.

When I look at the ministry of Jesus, I often tell myself, "That worked great for him, but I've got nothing compared to Jesus!" However, Jesus was persistent in reminding his disciples that they could expect to do similar works because they received the same Spirit. In addition, Jesus' ministry started with him simply reaching out to the people around him. He turned water into wine to spare a family embarrassment, healed Peter's mother-in-law, and cast out a demon in his local synagogue. All of these works took place among people he knew and in places he frequented.

We don't have to travel to far-off lands, wander the streets at night, or work for an official ministry to do the work of Jesus. We can pray for our friends and family today, we can share what we have with the neighbors around us who are in need, and we can pay attention to the people around us each day in our neighborhoods and workplaces to discern which ones need a friend to reach out to them. The power and influence of Jesus' ministry started like a tiny seed in the soil where he'd been planted in Galilee. As he focused on faithfully doing the work God placed before him each day, his "power" expanded.

Generosity of Power

Whatever power we have, God wants us to give it away and use it for the benefit of those who don't have power. This runs counter to the general consensus that power should be defended at all costs and consolidated when possible. Rather than consolidating his power, Jesus empowered his disciples to do the same miracles and to preach the same message. This wasn't the *Jesus Show* with his servants who propped up his ministry. He wasn't interested in keeping all of the influence and power to himself. If anything, his followers simply weren't ready to accept the kind of power he was giving. In fact, to them, his "power" felt like a demotion. Who among his followers wanted to wash feet, suffer persecution, put themselves last, or give away positions of power and influence?

Even if we spend time serving others, we can serve in a way that still maintains our power and control. We may even give the powerless the leftovers, so to speak. The kind of service that Jesus talked about served others by actually empowering them—healing, commissioning, and gently instructing. This wasn't just symbolic tithing.

As I've served among the poor and imprisoned, I've noticed that I can frequently let my perceptions about class affect the way I serve others. I'm happy enough to provide a meal or lead a Bible study, but am I willing to treat the people I'm serving as equals? Will I even let them speak into my own life? I prefer to keep my distance as the one who is serving. But the generosity of Jesus includes being generous with power, letting new Christians pray for their "mentors." This means working alongside the poor and letting them guide our projects without creating a savior complex for ourselves. If you feel like you're losing control, then you're probably doing it right, and that is why practicing the generosity of Jesus is so hard.

AN ALL-POWERFUL AND COMPLETELY CONFUSING GOD

The way God uses power may continue to be among the most difficult puzzles in the Bible. In particular, theologians have puzzled for centuries over the "problem of evil" in a world with an all-powerful God. If anything, Jesus suggests that we are just scratching the surface in our understanding of how God uses power. When we speak of a sovereign or all-powerful God, we could be misunderstanding the nature of God's power and influence. Perhaps the term *soft power* could offer us an imperfect but useful correction. Jesus exerted his power by healing and literally touching others. He didn't challenge the rulers of his time in a head-on confrontation; rather he stuck to the margins of society and offered would-be followers an invitation to join his kingdom. This soft power is a notable contrast to the steel power of Herod and Pilate that relied on fear, intimidation, coercion, and violence.

However we speak of Jesus' power, he used his power to build God's kingdom, a place where the last come first, the poor are blessed, the humble rule the earth, and those who mourn receive comfort. In contrast to anything else we can build today, the kingdom of God endures, blesses, and offers the kind of hope and change our world is longing to experience.

As Martin Luther hid in a castle in Germany, he saw the ways power brought corruption and destruction. Even his homeland would be ravaged by a peasant revolt against the German rulers. He had many opportunities to see the breakdowns that occur when rulers and people grapple for control and influence. You could even argue that he benefited directly or indirectly from these struggles. As he approached his final days, Luther knew about the emptiness of power and influence in this world. While historians may help us remember Luther's many accomplishments, the most enduring is also the most important: a gracious God who saves people by faith because he humbly defeated death and rose from the grave in a display of power the world had never seen before and has never seen since.

NOTE

1. For an accessible survey of the images and symbols Jesus used in relation to political power, see Shane Claiborne and Chris Haw, *Jesus for President: Politics for Ordinary Radicals* (Grand Rapids, Mich.: Zondervan, 2008).

■9 CAIAPHAS

A MESSIAH WHO LEAVES US IN CHARGE

Some of the earliest stories recorded by humanity explain the creation of the world and human origins. For example, the Babylonian creation myth, known as Enuma Elish, tells the grisly story of Marduk's battle with the rival goddess, Tiamat. After Marduk defeated his foe, he used her body to create the world. While it's hard for us to imagine what exactly the Babylonians made of this story, it at least answered the most basic question: What is the origin of humanity?

The Bible provides us with another origin story that provides a far less harrowing creation event. Rather than ripping apart a rival god, Yahweh created the world on his own and provided order to a shapeless world. Humanity was created to be a companion and caretaker until choosing to gain knowledge of good and evil like a god. We once again learn where we came from and why things are the way they are.

Origin stories are still extremely popular today. When we cross into the contemporary world, we find that origins are essential in mythical, historic, and literary works—even comic books. Origins are important because we need to know where a hero comes from and what drives the hero, but we also need to know why the hero has an enemy. If we don't know what's at stake or if there's no inciting incident that sends the villain on a collision course with the hero, the villain's actions fall flat, taking on the appearance of madness. The story doesn't work unless we know what drives the hero and villain.

TWO MEN WHO TRIED TO SAVE ISRAEL

When we meet Caiaphas in the Gospels, he emerges as the ringleader of the Sanhedrin who decides that it's best for the people that Jesus dies, but he didn't start out as a murderous high priest. Caiaphas has his own origin story as one of the Bible's leading villains.

When the Romans took control of Israel, they meddled in the selection of the high priest. The Jews were waiting for a messiah to come and serve as prophet, priest, and king. By appointing separate kings and priests, the Romans took care of that expectation. Caiaphas married into the high priesthood, we may presume, by marrying the daughter of Annas, the high priest who preceded him. He served at the pleasure of the Romans, not his own people, meaning that Caiaphas lived in an uncomfortable tension. Though his office was politically necessary for the Romans, Caiaphas also recognized that any hint of rebellion could spell the doom of the Jewish people and his own fragile position. When Jesus arrived on the scene, Caiaphas had a lot to lose at the hands of a messiah.

The Rise of a Villain

Ironically, Caiaphas and Jesus shared the same goal: save the people of Israel. At the moment Jesus hung on the cross, both men believed they were saving Israel. Caiaphas thought he had prevented a Roman invasion that would have been instigated by the fledgling Jesus movement. Meanwhile, Jesus saved Israel from its sins, especially those caused by Caiaphas and his Roman collaborators.

Saying Caiaphas was a bad guy misses the point of the story. Caiaphas *became* a bad guy who still believed he was doing the best for his people—a public figure who had no idea what he was plotting—while keeping his position safe and sound. Caiaphas and the Sanhedrin attempted to prevent the Romans from destroying Jerusalem, but he became a terrible villain in the process. His story presents several ways that sin sneaks up on us, prevents us from experiencing God's salvation, and turns us into sin-twisted people in the process.

Americans struggle to relate to the oppression and heartbreak faced by the Israelites. Over two hundred years ago, when the British taxed our stamps, stuck some soldiers in each home, and shot a few civilians, our countrymen and women rose up in rebellion. Back in the time of Jesus, the Romans taxed the people into poverty and brutally executed anyone who rebelled. They exerted significant influence over the Jewish rulers, appointing everyone in a significant position.

Under the Roman occupation, the high priesthood in Israel wasn't exactly the same respected position once held by Aaron in Exodus. Recognizing an opportunity to create powerful sympathizers among the highest ranks of the Jewish people, the Romans meddled in the high priest selection process to the point that many Jews considered the new position a fraud. The Jewish people of Jesus' day were quite divided in their opinions, and Caiaphas and his fellow leaders were more of a puppet government than legitimate representatives of the people. Many Jews no doubt resented, if not opposed, everything Caiaphas stood for. When we make a historical remark that Caiaphas and the Sanhedrin plotted the death of Jesus along with the Roman governor, we're talking about a small, elite group that in no way represented the will of the average person at the time of Jesus. Caiaphas and the Sanhedrin feared a riot, a clue that suggests the popularity of Jesus, even if his band of committed followers remained quite small. Caiaphas rightly viewed his position of authority as tenuous due to the opposition to his power.

The Jewish elites like Caiaphas tried to keep one foot in both worlds. To a person like Caiaphas, the taint of his Roman sponsorship could be written off as a minor occupational hazard. As a cold pragmatist, Caiaphas was just trying to make something work under the less-than-ideal reality of Roman military occupation. At the very least, the people of Israel could live in their own land and worship at their temple—the possible loss of which troubled the chief priests and Pharisees in John 11. Though the Romans taxed the Jewish people into poverty and brutally killed any suspected of rebellion, Caiaphas could always say, "At least we're not in exile." If anything, Caiaphas saw himself as maintaining an uneasy truce so that the Messiah could come and deliver Israel.

Straddling two worlds is never easy, and it's only human nature to expect one world to triumph over the other. Pragmatists like Caiaphas can't sit back and watch a problem develop. They think of solutions and take definitive steps toward solutions. In the case of Caiaphas, we see that the values of one world began to trump those of the other when Jesus came onto the scene.

Messiah Wanted: An Impossible Job Description

Besides managing tensions with Rome, Caiaphas also had a long checklist for the reasons why Jesus couldn't be the Messiah. Jesus broke the law, insulted the teachers of the law, scrapped the Jewish ceremonial customs, and refused to directly confront the Romans while hinting at his new kingdom. In the eyes of Caiaphas, Jesus was either a scheming trickster or a raving madman—either way, the solution required brutal action. The alternative to violence against Jesus was unthinkable: waiting for the Romans to destroy Israel.

As a religious authority, Caiaphas had a clear picture of what deliverance from God should look like. He had no intention of risking the stability of Israel for the sake of a false messiah. When Jesus raised Lazarus from the dead, Caiaphas and the Sanhedrin faced a volatile situation. If the Romans threatened to kill his followers, this Messiah could simply raise them from the dead. If the Romans besieged Jerusalem, this Messiah could multiply bread and fish. If they ran out of wine at the Messiah's coronation, they only needed a jug of water. Right up to his crucifixion, Jesus remained a popular figure among the public, alarming only a select few, such as Caiaphas. From the perspective of many people, Jesus performed enough miracles to convince them that he was at least a holy man from God, even if many were slow to believe that he was the Messiah. Caiaphas, however, along with most Jewish leaders, didn't see how a politically indifferent messiah who flaunted the authority of the Jewish leaders and the law could deliver Israel from Rome. From their perspective, Jesus had taken his little movement too far with the raising of Lazarus, and he had to be stopped.

Jesus represented the ultimate catch-22 for Caiaphas. The people saw him as a prophet, and if the Jewish leaders opposed him openly, the people could have revolted and brought down the wrath of Rome—the very thing feared among cities occupied throughout the Roman Empire. However, if Jesus continued his ministry, the people may revolt anyway and Israel would be destroyed. Caiaphas needed to cover his tracks so that he could prove himself as a law-abiding Jew, an Israelite patriot, and a friend of Rome. While he certainly expressed concern about the fate of Israel and the temple, Caiaphas and the Sanhedrin also wanted to protect their positions of authority. We have few examples from history of powerful leaders giving up their positions willingly, and when Jesus criticized the Jewish leaders, he pointed out their love for the seats of honor in the synagogues and the acclaim of the people in the market (Luke 11:43). Though Caiaphas may not have been the specific target of this passage from Luke, it's not too hard to imagine that he felt the same way about guarding his position as high priest.

Caiaphas hatched a plan that covered all his bases and ensured that he had all of the leverage he needed to kill Jesus, save his own position, and supposedly save Israel from Rome. All he had to do was twist the law of God to his own purposes. For starters, Caiaphas had to charge that Jesus had blasphemed God by claiming to *be* God. The penalty according to the law was death. However, the Sanhedrin couldn't kill Jesus on its own; therefore, they added the charge that Jesus had also claimed to be the king of the Jews—a treasonous statement against the rule of Rome that demanded death as well. Either way, Caiaphas could demonstrate that his hands were tied by the laws of Israel and Rome. Jesus had to die, and there was nothing Caiaphas could do to save him. However, as a way of playing to the national sentiments at that time, Caiaphas also accused Jesus of threatening to destroy the temple. Such an act was unthinkable to Jews back then. Pinning Jesus with a plot to destroy the temple would at least prevent a riot once the public heard about his conviction. Even if the people sympathized with Jesus as the possible Messiah, they would not riot for the sake of someone who had even hinted at destroying their temple.

The Rival Villain

If there is any comedy in the story of Caiaphas, it's supplied by Pontius Pilate. Pilate hated the Sanhedrin and tended to pursue the course opposite to the one they desired. If they wanted Jesus to die, Pilate wanted Jesus to live, dismissing him as a madman. Some readers see Pilate as acting somewhat compassionately toward Jesus. However, for someone in Pilate's position, with the fear of revolution at any moment, it was nothing to kill a single Jew who hinted at rebellion. Just as Pilate seemed to be on the verge of releasing Jesus, the Sanhedrin played their trump card: threatening to go over Pilate's head to report that he had refused to kill a dangerous revolutionary.

By the time Caiaphas mocked Jesus on the cross, we have a picture of how completely a high priest can turn away from God. With his temple secure and his position bolstered after besting

Pilate, Caiaphas demonstrated how utterly he had veered from the path of God, despite dedicating his life to observing the law and memorizing the Scriptures. Few people knew more than Caiaphas, yet he was among the most hardened, calloused sinners in the land. Hardly anyone knew what Caiaphas had orchestrated, and that was exactly how he wanted to keep it.

CAN WE LEARN ANYTHING FROM CAIAPHAS?

One of the hardest things for readers today to grasp is just how dangerous Jesus appeared to Caiaphas and the other elite Jewish leaders. For those of us who grew up with a flannelgraph Jesus, a smiling Savior who blesses children, it's hard to imagine Jesus as a dangerous revolutionary who could lead to the destruction of an entire nation. Today it's even more difficult to figure out what we stand to learn from a villain such as Caiaphas. We're so far removed from his priorities and values, it's hard to understand how he moved from political collaborator into murder conspirator, let alone learn something from him. It's fair of us to ask: What do we stand to learn from Caiaphas? Do we really have anything in common with him?

While I doubt anyone today is plotting anything as terrible as the conspiracy Caiaphas put together, he can demonstrate vices on such a scale that we can view them with unusual clarity. When we see them in a life such as Caiaphas's, we're able to step back and examine our own lives where these same vices may appear on a much smaller scale but where they may fester and threaten our growth and ministry.

On Straining Gnats and Swallowing Camels

In one of the more over-the-top scenes in the movie *Saved!* a group of Christian teens attempt an evangelistic intervention on a friend they fear may be falling away from the faith. At the height of the conflict, the main characters have the following exchange:

> HILARY FAYE: Mary, turn away from Satan. Jesus, he loves you.
>
> MARY: You don't know the first thing about love.
>
> HILARY FAYE: [throws a Bible at Mary] I am FILLED with Christ's love! You are just jealous of my success in the Lord.
>
> MARY: [Mary holds up the Bible] This is not a weapon! You idiot.[1]

In the midst of supposedly trying to win over a friend to a Savior who taught his followers to love one another, we see a group of aggressive, forceful evangelists completely missing the point of the Bible. Though this movie does not necessarily represent what often happens, the over-the-top nature of the scene taps into the ways religion can evolve into an us-versus-them conflict. Though sharing the gospel can be a very loving practice, it's surprisingly easy to do it in a very unloving way.

Caiaphas is a character who had remained close to the Jewish Law and still drifted away from its core teachings, seemingly obeying it while actually breaking it. For instance, let's start with a look at the solution Caiaphas proposed to his problem with Jesus. Caiaphas made a simple calculation: He could kill Jesus or the Romans could kill everybody, including Jesus. It was a simple math problem that suddenly made killing a man look like a small matter.

Ironically, Caiaphas and the Sanhedrin continued to try and follow the law to the letter while arranging to kill Jesus with Rome's help. They refused to enter Pilate's palace; they pleaded to have the "criminals" removed from their crosses before the Sabbath; and they properly disposed of the blood money that Judas had cast at their feet. The words of Jesus about the teachers of the law straining out a gnat and then swallowing a camel ring particularly true here (see Matt. 23:24). One of the reasons why Caiaphas remained deaf and blind to the message and practices of Jesus was his inability to connect with the heart of God in the midst of his religious observances.

As I look at this story, even though I certainly have not entangled myself with something as serious as a murder conspiracy, I can see that I have sometimes been consumed by the smaller details of Christianity and ignored the more important matters of love, mercy, and justice. Everything began to change when I started visiting prison inmates and serving meals at our local community center. I don't know how I could have missed the call of Jesus to selflessness and service to others. He spent his entire ministry healing, feeding, and teaching, but I had reduced him to merely a teacher who wanted to change what I thought and believed.

Compromise Catches Up with Us

Though we're left to speculate on some of Caiaphas's inner motivations throughout his encounters with Jesus, there is no doubt that we have a character with divided loyalties. Tragically, Caiaphas didn't realize how far he'd compromised his allegiance to God. Though he would have had no doubt that he was on the side of Israel's God, he ended up opposing the Messiah sent from the very same God. At some point in his life, Caiaphas radically departed from the central tenets of Judaism to love the Lord with all of his heart, mind, soul, and strength—how else could he have chosen so terrible a course in his life?

Caiaphas presents the ugliness of sin in full bloom, but we do him a grave disservice if we think he took office as an expert at murder conspiracies. Over time he grew attached to his authority, his dreams for Israel under his leadership, and the comfort he gained from his position as high priest. He tried to preserve the status quo, not realizing that his supposed support for a future messiah had become attached to the continuation of the current political situation that preserved the temple and his position. That Jesus could predict the destruction of the temple spelled national calamity and signaled the end of everything Caiaphas held dear. He feared the loss of the temple, the nation, and his position to the point that he was determined to protect them at any cost— even if he ended up fighting against God and violating the law.

Compromise is hard to detect. Caiaphas certainly knew the Old Testament Scriptures, and yet he veered so far from God's ways that he ended up framing the Messiah as a revolutionary. That should give us pause. Have we made any compromises against the ways of God that may send us away from God?

This is one of the tougher questions I'm forced to ask based on the story of Caiaphas, especially because it's often hard to see our own blind spots. I've had blind spots in areas that range from mixing politics and religion to failing to treat my neighbors with kindness. However, I can certainly identify with the need Caiaphas felt for security—both personally and monetarily. We all want to live in a location where we feel safe, and we all want to have enough money in the bank so that we can put food on the table and keep the lights on. However, these good things can quickly take on such an important position in our own lives that we begin to serve money and security rather than use them as God directs us and trust him for provision. Small compromises can add up quickly, allowing idols to take the place of God in our lives.

When we serve idols such as money, security, or power, we will be transformed by the power of sin rather than the power of the Holy Spirit. Before we realize it, we will be completely alienated from the influence of God in our lives, and we'll become slaves to our impulses and desires. At a certain point, we will choose between God and our idols. Caiaphas serves as an extreme case of just how badly sin can warp our thinking into believing that we are serving God when we are, in fact, serving ourselves.

What Caiaphas Expected God to Do

We all think we know what God can and cannot do. I used to be convinced that God doesn't perform miracles or any other kind of supernatural manifestation anymore. The first time I heard about the works of the Holy Spirit today, I thought about turning off the radio. Some preacher in Toronto started describing this sword that was flying through the air. It sounded a little fishy, and I wrote it off as something that he was just making up. Years later, I attended several charismatic churches for the first time, and I just about hid underneath a chair. People danced in the aisles with flags, others fainted, and one lady in front of me had a bag full of props, such as a toy sword that she waved around during worship.

My skepticism started to fade when the Holy Spirit showed up at a chapel service while I attended a Christian college. There was a widespread conviction of sin, and some of my friends doubled over weeping as they grasped God's forgiveness for their darkest sins. That caught my attention. One person after another stood at the microphone to publicly confess sins until the line streamed along the stage and down an aisle. I never heard a public wail of mourning until that moment. No one that I know of left sad that day. This time of repentance brought peace and joy as God began to set many free. The intense moments of grief were punctuated with renewed hope.

A few years after that, I received prayer on several occasions where those praying knew exactly what I was thinking and what was keeping me from God. It was my turn to confess my sins with weeping as God broke through my doubts and fears. In the years that followed, God began to speak to me. Sometimes I sensed that I needed to give someone money, and other times I had a specific word of hope or a prayer to share with someone. Healing or encouragement resulted every time I experienced the work of the Holy Spirit.

At the center of the story about Caiaphas is a bigger question about what God can and cannot do. There is a power struggle between God and a corrupt high priest. Before Caiaphas began to actually plot the death of Jesus, some assumptions had already taken root in his mind about what God is able to do, if anything. So far as I can tell from the snapshots we have of Caiaphas, he thought he had matters under control on his own without God's help. Caiaphas strikes me as the kind of person who wanted to handle his problems rather than waiting for God to supernaturally intervene.

That God could show up and perform miracles was certainly a shock to someone in Caiaphas's position. Caiaphas didn't recognize the potential of God intervening among his people, and that cut him off from the work of God in his day. On a lesser scale, we have a serious problem today when Christians deny the ability of the Holy Spirit to work among God's people and live as if they don't need God's power working in and through them. I've read about and witnessed abuses of the Holy Spirit by those who tried to claim a special word of knowledge from God only to advance a personal agenda. However, if we let these instances of abuse create a narrative where God cannot work among us, we may find ourselves resisting the genuine work of God someday, especially if we view every manifestation of his Spirit with criticism and unbelief. Humility is warranted when dealing with the work of the Holy Spirit today, as God may work in ways that surprise us.

The risk in discussing the pitfalls of Caiaphas is that it could sound like I'm creating an overdramatic comparison that has nothing to do with today. Provided we realize that Caiaphas offers a worst-case scenario illustration of sin, we can clearly spot the tracks of sin and then look for the same clues when we examine our own lives. I've had my doubts of the Holy Spirit in the past, but I was never in danger of becoming like Caiaphas. We can see that doubt of the Holy Spirit is clearly destructive in the life of Caiaphas, but we may go easy on ourselves. Caiaphas reminds us that alienation from God will drag us to some dark places, and we must seek God's leading in our lives with everything we have or else we may start fighting against God.

A NEW ORIGIN STORY

By understanding the origin story of Caiaphas, we can see the making of a villain. As it turns out, the ingredients that go into a villain are common problems we all face: divided loyalties, an inability to change course, and a flawed view of vices and virtues.

Caiaphas managed to let his position, religious expectations, and twisted religious practices cut himself off from his long-awaited messiah. However, today, disciples face these same dangers — we just deal with them on a smaller scale.

There are plenty of opportunities to let other priorities trump the call of Jesus. We can easily place God in a box and end up ignoring or opposing the work he's doing today. It's conceivable that we could obey the easy parts of Christianity while leaving the more difficult aspects untouched.

The story of Caiaphas is in the Gospels for a reason. He serves as the greatest warning to disciples about the many ways God's people can lose their way. If the story of John the Baptist leaves us surprised that a prophet could doubt the direction of God in his life, Caiaphas should leave us humbled that a priest so close to the Scriptures could end up violating them so dramatically.

Caiaphas also reminds us that he isn't the true villain in the Bible. The true villain lurks in our own lives, threatening us each day. More than any one person, sin is a cancer that can take over our lives if allowed to grow and flourish. We may not turn into a Caiaphas, but he reminds us that sin can drag us to places we would have never imagined. For those willing to wait for God to show up on his own terms, they will find a God who honors their loyalty, reshapes them with love, and guides them to serve others. We are never left without hope in our struggle with sin. Perhaps the story of Caiaphas can become part of our own origin stories — the ones where we choose to take a firm step away from sin so that God's Spirit can begin the work of renewal today.

NOTE

1. "*Saved!* Quotes," Internet Movie Database, accessed February 9, 2012, http://www.imdb.com/title/tt0332375/quotes.

■10 THE EMMAUS DISCIPLES

A MESSIAH WHO SURPRISES US

Sundar Singh was on track to become a religious leader among the Sikh people of northern India in the early 1900s. His piety coupled with his knowledge of the Sikh holy book and the Hindu holy book made him renowned throughout his region by the time he reached his teens. His mother had also enrolled him in a Christian high school so he could learn English, but he looked to a local holy man for his religious instruction.

Tragedy struck Singh at a young age when his mother suddenly died. As he mourned her death, he denounced God and even went so far as publicly ridiculing Christians. He purchased a Bible and burned it page by page. Each of the three religions around him, Sikhism, Hinduism, and Christianity failed to speak to the emptiness he felt. Singh then resolved to spend three last days seeking God. If unsuccessful, he would kill himself by laying his head on the train tracks in the early morning darkness as the 5 a.m. train rolled through his town.

A bright light filled his room at 4:45 a.m., and Singh saw Jesus. This took him completely by surprise, but he immediately resolved to become a Christian. Upon learning this news, Singh's father disowned him and his own brother tried to poison him. Fleeing for his life, Singh took shelter among the Christians in his town. After struggling to fit in at an Anglican seminary, Singh adopted the turban and yellow robe of a local holy man, a sadhu, and began an intense itinerant ministry throughout northern India and southern Afghanistan preaching about Jesus. Singh was warmly welcomed by his own people because he shared the gospel without the British trappings of colonialism. It is widely reported that Singh had visions of Christ and even performed miracles, though he downplayed the latter as a safeguard against pride.

Singh preached the gospel throughout the world, but he ultimately desired to take his message to the unreached region of Tibet—the very place that remained most hostile to him. In a previous visit, people had attempted to stone him. After spending several years compiling some of his most important teachings, Singh set out for what would be his final preaching trip. His friends saw him walk into the foothills of Tibet and never heard from him again.[1] While it is tragic that Singh's life most likely ended prematurely, he took great comfort in knowing that God found him, loved him despite his history of persecuting Christians, and gave him a mission to perform. His life had hung in the balance, just a few steps away from the train tracks. At the peak of his despair, Jesus showed up and taught him an important lesson: that he had been there all along.

THE ROAD AWAY FROM JESUS

The story of the resurrection shows God's people moving from the depths of despair to the hope of new life. Hard days remained for them, but with the promise of God going with them, they were able to endure. There is no formula for the way God works in the midst of hard times. For every story like Sundar Singh's, there's another one where calamity struck someone's life and nothing seemed to work out quite right. However our lives unfold, there's something we can relate to in the story along the road to Emmaus. We've all had moments when we've doubted or wanted to run away from God. The Emmaus story suggests that God may be closer than we think.

When All Is Lost

After the death of Jesus, Jerusalem was the last place a follower of Jesus would want to be. If the Jewish rulers were bold enough to kill Jesus, what would they do with his disciples? Everyone was liable to persecution and even death, and the disciples hid in a locked upper room to keep out of trouble. As we read Luke's report that two disciples departed for the nearby village of Emmaus (Luke 24:13), we can't blame them for making a break for it. Placed in their shoes, most of us would be with them.

It's hard for us to fathom the heartbreak and discouragement of these two men. They were no doubt among the crowds who waved palm branches the week before as Jesus entered Jerusalem. They probably listened to Jesus teach in the temple and might have eaten with him and asked him questions about the nature of God's kingdom. They expected deliverance from their enemies and recognized that Jesus was a powerful prophet. To their crushing disappointment, Rome and the Jewish high council put an end to all of their hopes.

Their hope for the future vanished. They couldn't imagine that God had anything else in store for them. What else could God do? If even the supposed messiah couldn't defeat the power of Rome and the Sanhedrin, what hope did anyone have? They needed time to process all that had happened. Where had they gone wrong? Would God send someone else to save Israel?

As we feel the weight of these questions for people who had waited from one generation to another for a messiah, we can imagine their shock that a traveling companion along the road had no idea what they were talking about. This was the focus of their lives. How could someone not wonder about whether Jesus was the Messiah?

Failing Messiah 101

The two disciples were familiar with Jesus. They had seen his miracles and heard his teachings about his impending death. They may have even puzzled over Jesus' statements about being raised after three days. With all that they had witnessed and heard from Jesus, his death still left them confused and despairing. How could Jesus raise a man from the dead and then die on the cross?

If there was ever a crisis of faith, this was it. Jesus couldn't be the Messiah if Rome could kill him. From what we can tell, these two men failed to believe what Jesus had predicted about himself.

When a stranger walked along and rebuked them for having so little faith, they surely would have struggled over what to think. Everything about Jesus had made sense at one point. Then it all fell to pieces. And now a man suggested that they had been right all along, just not in the way they expected. They had thought Jesus was the Messiah for the wrong reasons, so it's no wonder that they had walked away after the death of Jesus. Their kind of messiah couldn't save through loss and death.

As this stranger connected the dots throughout Scripture, explaining the role of Jesus as the Messiah, something happened. Their hearts started beating with excitement. Before they knew exactly what to think about Jesus, they started to feel that something about Jesus had to be true.

Feeling Faith

At the start of their journey, these two disciples were thinking through the ways Jesus could or couldn't be the Messiah. They discussed the events of the past few days over and over again. They no doubt recited all that Jesus taught and tried to piece together some sort of sense based on the passages of Scripture they could remember. All of their best thinking couldn't piece together a way to make sense of the Scriptures, the ministry of Jesus, and their hopes for a messiah.

It may surprise us that Jesus would go out of his way to reach out to these two doubting disciples running away from Jerusalem. Shouldn't he have focused on the group of disciples praying in the upper room? Jesus clearly saw something he could work with in these two men. They were willing to keep struggling with the pieces in front of them even as they ran away.

As Jesus opened their minds to the Scriptures, the two disciples started to sense that Jesus really could be the Messiah. What their minds were slow to sort out, their hearts discerned. They felt the uniqueness of Jesus before they could explain it.

In a beautiful moment sharing a meal together, everything finally made sense. As Jesus blessed the bread and broke it in their presence, they were both restored to fellowship with Jesus and intellectually clued in to his identity. What they had sensed in their hearts, they finally grasped with their minds as they sat down to eat with Jesus.

This theme of restoration through a meal played out in other situations as well. When Jesus appeared to Peter and the other disciples along the Sea of Galilee, he invited them to join him for breakfast. Jesus recommissioned Peter and the other disciples over a meal. Much like the disciples in Galilee, the two disciples on their way to Emmaus were finally brought back to Jesus by breaking bread together.

Rather than sending away these unfollowers, Jesus reached out to them again and ate with them. He gave them every chance to go their own way. He even resisted their invitation at first. But they had felt something while talking to this man. They had been convinced about Jesus. They wanted to learn more from this stranger and invited him into their home. They wanted him to be a part of their lives. As they responded to the truth they'd sensed in their hearts, they were also responding to Jesus.

Jesus joined these disciples who teetered on the brink of unbelief for a meal. He wasn't about to let them slip away. He knew they were spiritually hungry, so he gave them the sign they needed as he broke bread with them. When they realized the man had been Jesus, they hurried back to Jerusalem to tell the other disciples. Death at the hands of the Romans or Jewish leaders no longer concerned them. Jesus was alive! He was the Messiah after all. He had overcome their doubts and found them when they ran away.

BELIEVING IN AN IMPOSSIBLE GOD

A Dead End for Faith

When I talk to friends and colleagues who have left the Christian faith, I regularly hear stories about trying and failing to make sense of God in the midst of tragedy or difficult circumstances. One couldn't find God after a school shooting. Another couldn't believe that God would prompt Christians to alienate homosexuals. Yet another endured several family tragedies where she just couldn't see a place for a caring God. I would guess that if you haven't had a crisis of faith, there's one coming in your future.

I can't say exactly why some believe, while others don't. The best I can offer is that in the midst of hard times in my own family, I have found Jesus most present. As alcohol turned a close relative into a monster, as my grandmother struggled to take her last breaths, and as my dear Catholic grandfather argued with me over my Protestant faith before he passed away, I've found Jesus palpably present. I don't believe God engineers tragedy, but nonetheless, we are left with uncomfortable questions when the worst happens in our lives. There is much we could say, and the only place to begin is discussing the presence of God in the midst of suffering and doubt—a presence that is real even when we're not aware of it. Many times I have sensed God's presence when I least expected it or had done next to nothing to seek him. He just showed up. Other times I've had to cling to the promises of Scripture. Whether you feel the presence of God or you feel like your faith is about to collapse, this story offers us a word of encouragement. Jesus won't abandon us—even if we have doubts and hard questions for a season. The trouble is that we don't always see him walking with us.

There are moments in our lives when faith in God will appear impossible. Whether that's a loss of a loved one, a national tragedy, or a difficult family relationship, our world is far from what God desires for his good creation. We may not know how to recover our faith in God when tragedy strikes. The question "why" is a persistent thorn in our side, and we may never have a clear answer that relieves the pain. Whether we doubt or we cling to belief, Jesus has saved us a place at his table. He's patient and kind. He can give us enough to sustain us, even if he doesn't give us everything we desire.

More than offering answers or deliverance from every trouble, the Emmaus story shows us that God has conquered death and can raise the dead to new life. There is something just over the horizon for us that God is preparing. I wonder if I sometimes become so fixated on finding clarity now that I forget how much is obscured in this life and how much will be revealed one day in God's presence. The hope of the gospel has never been easy answers, solutions to every problem, or even healing from every disease. Jesus faced death ahead of us and can deliver us from the finality of our last breaths because the new life we've received in him will keep going and will even be fully revealed one day. The Emmaus disciples were just at the start of their journey.

Facts Are Not Faith

It's common for seminary students to have a crisis of faith after graduation. At least the former seminary students I know. There is a great deal to learn about Jesus and the Bible, but facts don't necessarily guarantee a thriving faith. It's possible to get all of the facts straight and still miss out on the love of God for his people.

After graduating from seminary, I struggled with the way people treated me. I'd often be asked to pray over a meal or to counsel someone in a crisis of faith. At the height of my theological knowledge, I was more uncertain than ever about my faith. I even went as far as hiding all of my seminary books upstairs so our friends wouldn't know about my time in seminary. My pastor had warned me that seminary would not supply all of the answers, and he was absolutely correct. I expected Christianity to become completely clear, but seminary only revealed to me that I'd put my faith in the wrong things: perfectly understanding the Bible and getting really involved in my church. Both fell short of providing the connection with Jesus that I longed for. In the years that followed seminary, I eventually found a better balance between my inner prayer life and my study of Scripture.

On my worst days as a Christian, I find the Emmaus story comforting. They got Jesus' story perfect because they witnessed it, but they still couldn't discern his true identity based on the facts alone. They needed his spiritual help to set themselves straight.

Jesus knew there would come a day when his followers would have to rely on eyewitness accounts and the presence of the Holy Spirit. He knew that faith and unity would be challenging. And yet, even with every advantage, plenty of disciples ended up on the fence about Jesus: "We thought he was the one, but things didn't work out." If the eyewitnesses couldn't get it right, we shouldn't be surprised to learn that some folks today read the Gospels and walk away feeling more confused and undecided than before. The facts of the Christian faith are important, but they aren't the whole story. In fact, the point of the story is that we get to live and participate in it. We aren't just students of Jesus who learn. We're expected to experience Jesus and to let him shape our lives through the experience of him. That may come in a quiet moment of prayer or it may come while sharing Communion with a congregation.

Are we willing to spend time waiting on the Lord, asking for him to give us wisdom and clarity? Maybe we're not experiencing God because we need to learn how to wait and listen better.

THE GREAT SURPRISE: JESUS LIVES AMONG US

For all of the times we doubt and are slow to believe, we should take comfort in the placement of the Emmaus story in Luke's gospel. Luke wanted us to know that even after reading all of his carefully researched stories about Jesus, some may still doubt. To our surprise, we'll find Jesus walking alongside us on the road. How long has he been there?

Christians may struggle with pride, love of money, doubts, false expectations for God, and busy schedules—and we can certainly let any of these things keep us from God. The unfollowers of Jesus throughout the Gospels show us that each of these things can become huge problems for disciples. Jesus reminds us in Luke that these obstacles to faith don't have to win out. He's right there with us, walking alongside us, just waiting for us to ask him a question.

We may need time to sort out confusion, to work through our doubts, and to let go of our past failings. We may take wrong turns along the way, completely missing the point of Jesus sometimes. Our theology may be wrong. We could let distractions throw us off the path or make terrible choices. Through it all, Jesus is able to teach and guide those willing to come to him for a new start.

Perhaps we imagine an angry or indifferent Jesus in the Gospels. It's hard to get a sense of his heart for people just by reading text on a page. Isn't Jesus bitterly disappointed by the lack of faith among the people in Jerusalem?

We get a better idea of Jesus' true thoughts when he looked down on Jerusalem, while the Jewish high council plotted his death, and wept. Jesus didn't shake his fist in the air and kick at rocks. While none of us would blame him for being angry, disappointed, or even vengeful, he walked to his death with tears of pity running down his face, saying, "Jerusalem, Jerusalem, you who kill the prophets and stone those sent to you, how often I have longed to gather your children together, as a hen gathers her chicks under her wings, and you were not willing" (Matt. 23:37).

He could have given up on the two disciples walking along the road to Emmaus. We could imagine Jesus saying, "Nope, I give up on these two. They're just not going to figure it out." Instead, he walked with them and broke bread at their table. Jesus knows that so many things can get in the way of following him, but he's still reaching out to us.

Does that shock you? Does it seem unlikely? Can you think of reasons why that could be true for others but certainly not for you?

Just as the unfollowers of Jesus came from a variety of backgrounds, so too did his followers. There were Jewish leaders, rabbis, common laborers, Roman soldiers, the wives of wealthy officials, and radical revolutionaries among Jesus' unlikely band of followers. They were liars, thieves, and skeptics. All who were willing to come were welcomed with open arms.

We learn from the stories of the unfollowers about the obstacles that can keep us from following Jesus, but the good news is that obstacles aren't the end of the story. The cross and the resurrection have removed every barrier that could keep us from God. The path is wide open. The choice to follow Jesus is ours to make.

He's spreading a table before us where we can sit down with him. We are his sons and daughters, brothers and sisters. He loves us enough to let us go our own way, but he wants nothing more than to welcome us at his table. He's breaking a loaf of bread and sharing it with us because he wants us to join his family. He's asking you to follow him.

NOTE

1. Details for this story were found in Richard Foster and James Bryan Smith, eds., *Devotional Classics: Selected Readings for Individuals and Groups* (San Francisco: Harper, 1993), 308–313.

APPENDIX

The following charts provide an overview of the unfollowers mentioned in the Gospels.

Unfollowers in the Synoptic Gospels			
Passage	**Group or Person**	**Location**	**Reason for Rejecting Jesus**
Matthew 2:1–18	Herod	Jerusalem or Bethlehem	Herod was fearful of people believing that Jesus was the "king."
Matthew 8:18–22; Luke 9:57–62	Individuals	Galilee	One person was fearful of not having a home, one of wanting to bury his father first, and the other wanted to say good-bye to his family first.
Matthew 8:27–34; Mark 5:1–20; Luke 8:26–29	People in the Gadarenes	Decapolis	They were fearful of Jesus' power to destroy their pig herd and change the demon-possessed man into a sane and normal person.
Matthew 9:10–13; Mark 2:15–17; Luke 5:29–32	Pharisees	Capernaum	Jesus was eating with sinners and tax collectors.
Matthew 9:14–17; Mark 2:18–20; Luke 5:33–39	John's disciples and Pharisees	Capernaum	Jesus did not fast like John's disciples and the Pharisees, but rather attended parties and appeared to be a glutton and drunkard.
Matthew 9:32–34; Luke 11:14–22	Pharisees	Galilee	Jesus cast out a demon from a man who could not speak, and the Pharisees reasoned that he only did this by the power of the Devil.

continued

Unfollowers in the Synoptic Gospels *continued*			
Passage	**Group or Person**	**Location**	**Reason for Rejecting Jesus**
Matthew 11:2–15; Luke 7:18–28	John the Baptist	Possibly Judea	John was unsure about Jesus' tactics and actions.
Matthew 11:16–19; Luke 7:31–35	This generation	Possibly Galilee	The people were criticizing Jesus for eating and drinking freely and also dining with sinners and tax collectors.
Matthew 11:20–24; Luke 10:13–15	Townspeople	Lakefront towns	These towns rejected Jesus' miracles.
Matthew 12:1–8; Mark 2:23–28; Luke 6:1–5	Pharisees	Cornfields	Jesus' disciples were "doing work" by picking ears of corn and eating them on the Sabbath.
Matthew 12:9–14; Mark 3:1–6; Luke 6:6–11	Pharisees	Synagogue	Jesus cured a man with a withered hand on the Sabbath.
Matthew 12:22–32; Mark 3:23–30; Luke 11:14–15, 17–23	Pharisees	Possibly Galilee	Jesus cured a man who was possessed by a demon, and the Pharisees said he could only cast out the demon since he was possessed with a demon himself. (See Matt. 9:32–34.)
Matthew 12:38–42; Mark 8:11–12; Luke 11:29–32	Scribes and Pharisees	Possibly Galilee	They wanted to see Jesus perform a "sign."
Matthew 12:46–50; Mark 3:31–35; Luke 8:19–21	Jesus' family	Possibly Galilee	Jesus' family thought he was crazy and wanted him to be silenced.
Matthew 13:53–58; Mark 6:1–6; Luke 4:16–30	People in Jesus' hometown	Nazareth	They did not think that Jesus could perform miracles, be the Messiah, or be a prophet since they had grown up with him.
Matthew 15:1–20; Mark 7:1–13	Pharisees and scribes from Jerusalem	Possibly Galilee	Jesus allowed his disciples to break away from the tradition of the elders, namely, by not washing their hands before eating.
Matthew 16:1–12; Mark 8:11–21	Pharisees and Sadducees	Possibly Galilee	They requested a sign from heaven.
Matthew 19:16–26; Mark 10:17–27; Luke 18:18–28	Rich young ruler	Possibly Galilee	The man did not want to give up his wealth, privilege, and power.
Matthew 21:12–27; Mark 11:15–33; Luke 19:45–46; 20:1–8	Those in temple, chiefly the priests	Jerusalem	They rejected Jesus' authority to "cleanse" the temple and rejected the implications of his message about Gentiles.

continued

Unfollowers in the Synoptic Gospels *continued*			
Passage	**Group or Person**	**Location**	**Reason for Rejecting Jesus**
Matthew 21:33–46; Mark 12:1–12; Luke 20:9–19	Priests and scribes	Jerusalem	They understood Jesus' cryptic story (parable) about the landowner rejecting and overthrowing the tenants.
Matthew 22:15–22; Mark 12:13–17; Luke 20:20–26	Pharisees	Jerusalem	They wanted to trap Jesus by getting him to say something controversial about taxes in relation to Rome, since they wanted a way to convict and kill him.
Matthew 22:23–33; Mark 12:18–27; Luke 20:27–40	Sadducees	Jerusalem	They rejected the resurrection and thought Jesus' teaching on the subject was ridiculous.
Matthew 22:34–40; Mark 12:28–31; Luke 10:25–28	Pharisees	Jerusalem	They wanted to trap Jesus into saying something that opposed the Torah.
Matthew 22:41–46; Mark 12:35–37; Luke 10:25–28	Pharisees	Jerusalem	They wanted Jesus to say something that proved that he could not be the Messiah.
Matthew 23:1–36	Pharisees and scribes	Jerusalem	Jesus condemned them for essentially being hypocrites who taught well but did not practice what they preached.
Matthew 26:14–16	Judas	Jerusalem	Judas was greedy and sought wealth.
Matthew 26:57–68; Mark 14:53–65; Luke 22:54–55, 66–71	Caiaphas the high priest and Sanhedrin	Jerusalem	They wanted to execute Jesus for his teachings, authority, and miracles.
Matthew 27:11–26; Mark 15:2–15; Luke 23:2–5, 13–25	Pontius Pilate	Praetorium in Jerusalem	Pilate was ignorant and afraid of the Jewish accusations against Jesus.
Matthew 27:27–31; Mark 15:16–20	Gentile soldiers	Jerusalem	They mocked Jesus and thought he was an insignificant Jewish charlatan.
Matthew 27:39–44; Mark 15:29–32; Luke 23:35–37	Jewish passersby	Jerusalem	They ridiculed Jesus as a false prophet.
Matthew 28:11–15	Gentile guards and chief priests	Jerusalem	The Jewish leaders bribed the soldiers, telling them to say that Jesus' body was stolen by his disciples.
Matthew 28:17	Jewish disciples	Galilee	Some of the eleven disciples "doubted" that Jesus really was the Messiah, perhaps because his appearance after the resurrection was questioned.

Unfollowers in the Gospel of John			
Passage in John	Group or Person	Location	Reason for Rejecting Jesus
2:19	Judeans	Jerusalem	Demanded a sign from Jesus for his cleansing of the temple.
5:1–47	Judeans	Jerusalem	Jesus cured a man, specifically on the Sabbath.
6:22–66	Judeans, people, and many of Jesus' disciples	Capernaum	Jesus taught that the people should eat his flesh and drink his blood, which was seen as blasphemous.
7:1–9	Jesus' brothers	Galilee	They did not believe in Jesus' messiahship—no doubt because they grew up with him as their brother.
7:14–24	Judeans	Jerusalem	Jesus was unlearned and uneducated.
7:25–30, 40–52	People	Jerusalem	Jesus was perceived as coming from Galilee, from which place no messiah would come—since Bethlehem was the place.
8:13–30	Pharisees	Jerusalem	Jesus was perceived as giving testimony only on his own behalf, rather than having testimony from others.
8:31–59	Judeans	Jerusalem	Jesus was blaspheming by teaching that the father of the people was actually the Devil, since they rejected his testimony. Jesus also blasphemed by teaching that he existed even before Abraham did.
9:1–41	Pharisees	Jerusalem	Jesus cured a blind man on the Sabbath. The family was afraid because they thought they would be excommunicated from the synagogue.
10:1–21	Judeans	Jerusalem	Jesus was teaching that he was the gatekeeper of the sheep, the Great Shepherd, that he had other sheep, and that he would lay down his life for his sheep.
10:22–39	Judeans	Jerusalem	Jesus was blaspheming by making himself out to be equal with God.
11:45–54; 12:9–11	Chief priests and Pharisees	Bethany and Jerusalem	Jesus brought Lazarus back from the dead.
12:1–8	Judas Iscariot	Bethany	Jesus allowed Mary, Lazarus's sister, to use a very expensive perfume on Jesus' feet rather than selling it and distributing the money to the poor.
12:37–41	Judeans	Jerusalem	God had prophetically blinded the eyes of those who rejected Jesus.
13:1–30	Judas Iscariot	Jerusalem	God had not "chosen" Judas, and the Devil had entered into him to lead him astray.

continued

Unfollowers in the Gospel of John *continued*			
Passage in John	Group or Person	Location	Reason for Rejecting Jesus
18:12–27	Annas and Caiaphas	Jerusalem	They could not accept Jesus' teachings or the origin of his disciples (and himself).
18:28—19:16	Pilate	Jerusalem	Pilate did not understand the nature of Jesus' teaching or origin, in addition to him being fearful of a riot and of word getting back to Rome that he let someone who claimed to be a king and god go unpunished.